MW00562743

Financial Planning
For Teachers

FINANCIAL PLANNING FOR TEACHERS

THE LESSON PLAN FOR YOUR FINANCIAL FUTURE

Eric Nichols, CFP®, CLU®, RICP®, CRPC®

EWS Communications
Pottstown, PA
First Edition.
Copyright 2015 by Eric Nichols, CFP®, CLU®, RICP®, CRPC®
All Rights Reserved. No portion of this book may be used or reproduced in any man-
ner whatsoever without written permission from the publisher.
ISBN: 0692581618
ISBN 13: 9780692581612
Library of Congress Control Number: 2015919389
EWS Communications, Pottstown, PA

For my wonderful wife and sons

E ric Nichols is a registered representative who offers securities products through AXA Advisors, LLC (212) 314-4600), member FINRA/SIPC, an investment advisor representative who offers investment advisory products and services through AXA Advisors, LLC, an investment advisor registered with the SEC, and an agent who offers annuity and insurance products through AXA Network, LLC. CA Insurance License #: 0D09274. AXA Network conducts business in California as AXA Network Insurance Agency of California, LLC.

Individuals may transact business and/or respond to inquiries only in state(s) in which they are properly qualified.

AXA Advisors and its affiliates and associates do not provide tax or legal advice. This book is for informational purposes only and is not intended as legal, tax or investment advice. Please consult your tax and/or legal and other professional advisors regarding your particular circumstances.

The RICP® (Retirement Income Certified Professional®) designation is sought by financial services sales professionals whose focus includes clients planning for their retirement income. The designation's required curriculum is administered by The American

College in Bryn Mawr, PA, which is accredited by The Middle States Commission on Higher Education, Philadelphia, PA 19104. The mark RICP® is the property of The American College and may be used only by individuals who have successfully completed the initial and ongoing certification requirements for this designation. Complaints about a designee can be made by e-mail at Registrar@TheAmericanCollege.edu or by calling 888-263-7265. To verify a designee, visit http://www.designationcheck.com.

The CRPC® (Chartered Retirement Planning Counselor SM) designation is sought by financial services sales professionals whose focus includes clients preparing for or living in retirement. The designation's required curriculum is administered by The College for Financial Planning, a regionally-accredited institution accredited by the Higher Learning Commission, a member of the North Central Association. The College is a wholly owned subsidiary of Apollo Group, Inc., Phoenix, AZ. The mark CRPC is owned by the College for Financial Planning and is awarded to individuals who successfully complete the College's initial and ongoing designation requirements. For information regarding complaints against a designee, visit www.cffpdesignations.com/Designee/standards. AGE 106859, PPG-106859

Praise for "Financial Planning for Teachers"

"A truly simplified and informative guide to managing your wealth for anyone who works in education. This would be the first "tool" to purchase for an educator's 'financial toolbox.'"
-Retired Guidance Counselor

"An entertaining informative text that is sure to be used as a reference guide for financial planning. Eric Nichols' book has a remarkable ability of simplifying an overwhelming topic with humor and clarity. Mr. Nichols may have just written himself out of a job!"
-Middle School Teacher

"Eric's book is easy to read and understand. There is information in it for every stage of a teacher's life. I wish I had a copy of this when I was first starting out as a teacher!"
-High School French Teacher

"This book should be required reading for all educators. Eric explains the mysteries of personal finance understandably and engagingly."
-Retired School District Administrator

"Financial Planning for Teachers" is an excellent resource for the busy educator on investing for their future. The book is easy to read and most of all, informational. I encourage every educator to get their hands on this book!"
-School District Administrator

"This is a must-read book for anyone in the education field. In a field where it is vital to get the most out of every dollar of income, Eric is able to explain how to do just that in a manner that is understandable and relevant to educators just beginning their career to those approaching retirement."
-School District Administrator

"The perfect book for the teacher who wants to make sure that there is money for retirement."
-Retired High School Teacher

"Take yourself on an educational field trip into your retirement planning!"
-Retired Elementary School Teacher

"Reading this book was the perfect way to internalize the concept of retirement planning. I've heard this language through personal meetings, but this reading material was basic and concrete. I will refer to the information in this book often!"
-Retired Elementary School Teacher

"Easy, straightforward, and packed with useful information. This quick read is the lesson plan for financial awareness."
-School District Administrator

"I would recommend this book to anyone currently in the workforce. The author does an excellent job of keeping the information easy to read, relevant, and informative."
-School District Administrator

"This book is clear, concise, convincing and condensed enough for even the busiest of teachers to find time to read in its entirety - ideal for all educators whether in their first or last year of their professional careers."
-Retired High School Teacher

"A must read for all educators. This book helps you plan your financial life from A to Z. Enjoy!"
-Career and Technical School Administrator

TABLE OF CONTENTS

Praise for "Financial Planning for Teachers" · · · · · · · ix

Introduction-Read this First! · · · · · · · · · · · · · · · · ·xv

Section I   **Pre-Retirement Planning** · 1

Chapter 1   How to Create A Financial Plan· · · · · · · · · · · · · · · 3

Chapter 2   The Base of the Pyramid–Protection · · · · · · · · · · · · 8

Chapter 3   Retirement Accumulation Planning · · · · · · · · · · · 24

Chapter 4   Accumulation in Non-Retirement Accounts /
Intermediate Term Investing· · · · · · · · · · · · · · · · 54

Chapter 5   The Tip of the Pyramid – Planning
for the Fun Stuff· 63

Chapter 6   Estate Planning And Legal Issues · · · · · · · · · · · · · 65

Section I   **Conclusion** · **73**

Section II   **To Retirement... and Beyond!** · · · · · · · · · · · · · · · · · · **75**

Chapter 7   Expenses in Retirement · · · · · · · · · · · · · · · · · · · 77

Chapter 8   Income in Retirement· 93

Chapter 9   Planning for Sustainable Income
             Streams in Retirement ·109

Chapter 10 Legacy Planning and Estate Planning · · · · · · · · · · ·115

             Afterword· ·123

             About the Author ·125

Introduction-Read this First!

I 'd like to start this book with a brief overview of what it is meant to be and why I decided to write it. I've spent over ten years working almost exclusively with educators and their families regarding their financial strategies. Over that decade I've been exposed to every imaginable type of financial situation, family situation, personality, set of goals, etc. If I haven't seen it all, I've come pretty close to it. At this point in my career I work primarily with what I would classify as "affluent and high net worth educators and their families." Now at this point you are probably laughing to yourself, thinking "high net-worth teacher, yeah right!" But then you might think about it a little more and realize that there actually are a good amount of well to do educators out there. Educators are typically very well educated themselves, many with advanced degrees, and they tend to marry other educated professionals. This can create a situation where there is a solid, combined household income and the potential to accumulate wealth.

I started my career when I was just 21 years old, right out of college. So for my early years in the business, I worked with a lot of younger educators, and those who were either just getting started in their planning, or were only a couple years into it. I worked with teachers in urban school districts and with teachers in some of the highest paying and most privileged districts in the state. Over the years I have worked with well over 1000 educators and their families. I mention all of this background just so you, the reader, understands that not only have I had exposure to just about every kind of financial planning situation, I have more than likely sat down and planned with somebody just like you.

What I have seen over the years working with so many different teachers has allowed me to recognize an overarching common theme. Teachers are generally very intelligent and caring individuals who know that they need to plan for their futures but typically don't have the time or the desire to do it themselves. More times than not, teachers tell me that they realize the importance of planning, but would really rather find somebody whom they like and trust and let that person handle the planning for them. Great! I think that is a good idea. However, how do you know that the person you like and trust is competent? Are they putting your best interests first? This book is meant to be a basic manual to help you better understand and collaborate with your financial advisor.

IT IS NOT MEANT TO REPLACE A FINANCIAL ADVISOR. I cannot stress that enough. Financial planning can be very complicated and everybody has a different set of circumstances. There is no such thing as "one size fits all." However, after reading this book, you should have a basic understanding of how to create a financial plan, what is important and what isn't, and be financially literate enough so that you can speak the same language as your advisor and feel comfortable during the meetings. While it is not the main purpose of this book, it should also help you figure out if your advisor is competent and if he or she is making sound recommendations.

Over the years I have been told by countless clients that I should be a teacher because I tend to have a knack for explaining complicated topics in easy to understand, plain English. It is my paramount goal for this book to have that voice. I hope that you feel as if you and I are talking as if we are in a meeting. This is not meant to be a formal, boring textbook. This is meant to be fun (seriously!) and easy to read. With that in mind...here we go!

SECTION I

PRE-RETIREMENT PLANNING

This book is organized by two sections. Section I covers everything you need to know up to retirement. If you are younger and do not want to read Section II, that's fine. Just keep the book until you hit retirement age and by then all the information in Section II should be obsolete, just kidding- I think.

CHAPTER 1

HOW TO CREATE A FINANCIAL PLAN

U sually when I meet with a new client they have no idea how to go about creating a financial plan. I mean, everyone knows that they need to save for retirement, save for education for the kids, and protect themselves and their families from tragedy, but the biggest question is "what gets the priority?" What I mean by that is that there isn't a money tree in the back yard so if I get paid X each month and my expenses are Y and I am left over with Z, what do I do if Z isn't enough money to fully fund all of my responsibilities? What gets priority?

The first step of creating your financial plan is to find out what we are working with. This means creating a monthly cash flow statement and then a budget. The cash flow statement will give us an idea of how much money is currently left over at the end of the month and then we can adjust our expenses going forward with a budget. By the way, in my experience hardly anyone has a budget any more. They just spend what they make. And we wonder why nobody is prepared for retirement? So if you don't currently have a budget, don't feel bad. You are in good company. If you do currently have a budget, congratulations, you are a big step ahead.

You can create a very simple cash flow statement on a spreadsheet or even on a piece of loose-leaf. Heck, do it on the back of a cocktail napkin if you want– I won't judge. If you prefer, there is a good online calculator at www.educatedwealthstrategies.com.

The first line is your monthly income. Take your direct deposit amount, or net pay, and multiply it by two. If you get paid over 26 pays then there will be two months where you get an extra paycheck. Don't forget this. You can either divide those two extra paychecks over the other ten months to average the monthly pay, or you can treat them as a bonus in the months they are received. Different strokes, right? Ok, so now we have your monthly take home pay. If you work any other jobs, or have other income, don't forget to include this as well. Also, if you are married you need to include your spouse's take home pay, too. Ok, now add this all up. The sum is your monthly after tax income. Now we need to work on your monthly expenses. Start writing them all down: housing, transportation, clothing, food, entertainment, utilities, phone, internet, insurances, charitable, student loans, and other debt with monthly payments, etc. Ok, now add these numbers. This will give you your total monthly expenditure. Now cross your fingers and close your eyes for the next step. Subtract your expenses from your income. Ok, you'll probably have to open your eyes again to do this. Hopefully, there will be a positive number there. This will be your monthly free cash flow (monthly after tax income - monthly expenses = monthly free cash flow). If by chance this number is negative, you should work as hard as you can to pay off debt and adjust your lifestyle until the number becomes positive because at this point, you have negative free cash flow each month, and this is not sustainable for long. What should jump out at you immediately are large expenses. Some of them you might not be able to help. The mortgage or rent, for example, is typically one of the larger expenses. If you are currently paying student loans, they might be a big expense, same with daycare. You don't really have a lot of choice here, so grin and bear it. However, you may notice large numbers in entertainment, clothing, car payment, and eating out. This is where a budget will help you. If you could control those areas, you would increase your free cash flow. There are lots of sample budgets available for free online, so I won't reinvent the wheel here, but I do recommend that you compare a sample budget to what you are currently running to highlight any glaring issues. So assuming that you have positive free cash flow, how do we allocate it to create our financial plan?

THE FINANCIAL PLANNING PYRAMID

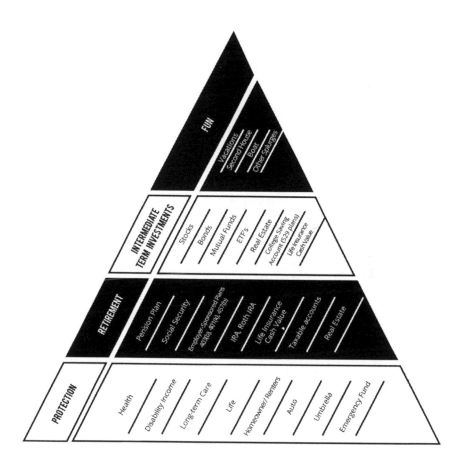

Most of you are probably familiar with the Food Guide Pyramid. I always chuckle when I think of the pyramid from when I was in grade school because I remember carbs being the biggest part of the pyramid, and now they are supposed to be the devil, right? Funny how things change. Anyway, I think one of the easiest ways to understand how to create a financial plan is to use a financial planning pyramid. There are many different versions and adaptations of this pyramid, and this is how I structure mine. As you can see, there are four levels. The bottom level of the pyramid contains the most important components to your financial plan. This level is primarily made of various insurance coverages and an emergency fund. The next level of importance is your long-term or retirement savings; typically consisting of pensions, 403(b) plans, 401(k) plans, IRAs and the like. The next level is your intermediate term savings, and the top level represents the "fat" from the food guide pyramid, or the fun things in life. In the next chapter we will dive into the bottom level of the pyramid; the protection parts of your plan.

Chapter 1 Points to Remember

- It is important to have an understanding of your monthly income and expenses
- A budget will help you see where your money is going and how to adjust going forward
- If your expenses are higher than your income you need to work to reduce expenses or pay off debt
- If your income is higher than your expenses, then we can start applying money to your financial plan
- The Financial Planning Pyramid is a useful tool to determine how to allocate dollars to your financial plan and what areas get priority

CHAPTER 2

THE BASE OF THE PYRAMID--PROTECTION

THE FINANCIAL PLANNING PYRAMID
(PROTECTION)

T he most important components to the plan are on the bottom level. These are your non-negotiables. You have to have them and they have to be adequate. These are your insurances and an emergency fund. So now you are thinking, "Insurance? When do we get to financial planning, you know, stocks, bonds, stuff like that?" Don't worry, we'll get there. What you need to know is even though insurance isn't as exciting as investments, it is far and away the most important part of your financial plan. I'll show you why. Your insurances are typically health, disability income, long-term care, life, auto, homeowners/renters, and an umbrella policy, which I strongly suggest.

Health Insurance:

As an educator, you probably have access to health insurance through your employer. It's rare that I've run across someone without it. Consider yourself lucky. There are a lot of Americans without good health insurance, and that can be a very scary situation. So why is it important and at the base of the pyramid? If you don't have health insurance and you get into an accident or get really sick you can kiss your savings and investments goodbye. Years of saving and investing for your future could be wiped out in a very short period given the exorbitant costs of medical care. It is not worth the risk. Health insurance comes in many types: HMO's, PPO's, high-deductible plans, etc. It's not in the scope of this book to go into the details, but to be as basic as possible, if you or your spouse have a choice in plans, if you have a lot of existing conditions and require a lot of medication and/ or go to the doctor a lot, you should probably pay a higher premium to get a plan with more coverage. On the flip side, if you are young and in "perfect health" and seldom need a doctor you might decide to go with a high deductible plan that has cheaper premiums. The bottom line, though, is that health insurance is essential to sound financial planning.

Disability Income Insurance:

Disability Income Insurance falls into two main fields, short-term and long-term. It's a good idea to review your contract and benefits to determine what coverage you have through your employer. A lot of people tend to think that since they have "disability income insurance" they are covered. Maybe, maybe not. You need to see if you have both short and long-term coverage. Short-term coverage will cover you for—you guessed it—short periods of time. Typical coverage lasts 3-6 months. This comes in handy if you become sick or injured with a temporary issue. You will receive a check from the insurance company to replace a portion of your income while you are on disability and watching TV all day in your pajamas. This certainly comes in handy, and I don't mean to slight it, but long-term disability income coverage is what is truly needed to avoid catastrophic financial ruin. This would typically come into play if you become paralyzed in an accident, lose your sight or hearing, or develop a disease that will not allow you to work (think along the lines of MS, cancer, arthritis, crippling back pain, heart attack, etc.) Long-term disability income coverage usually starts after about 90 days and may continue to pay benefits until around age 65. Please understand that there are many different kinds of long-term disability income policies with all kinds of different bells and whistles. It is really important for you to find out:

1) Do you have long-term disability income coverage through your employer?
2) If so, how much does it provide each month if you go on claim?
3) Does it have a cost of living adjustment (do you get a raise every year to keep pace with inflation)?
4) When do benefits end?
5) What is the definition of disability? Some policies do not pay benefits unless you are totally and completely disabled, so you basically cannot do any kind of work. This is a very strict definition of disability and is hard to achieve. By the way, this is

the definition of disability that Social Security uses. There are other definitions like "Own Occ" meaning own occupation. In this case you would collect benefits as long as you are disabled in such a way that you cannot work in your own occupation. This is much less stringent (and better for you).

6) Have you accumulated a large number of sick days? Do you participate in a "sick day bank" that could allow you to share others' accumulated sick days? What are the rules surrounding this?

7) Hey, Honey, what are your benefits at work? Don't forget your spouse if you are married!

If you or your spouse has less than ideal coverage or in some cases none at all, you should buy disability income coverage. This is where a good financial advisor or insurance advisor is worth their weight in gold. They can help you determine the best kind of coverage for your situation and shop different carriers for you.

In case I need to point it out, if you don't have disability income coverage and you get seriously sick or injured and cannot work, all of your savings and investments will be liquidated. You see, it's funny how we still need to eat and pay the bills, even when we can't work.

Long-term care Insurance:

Long-term care is not typically medical care but instead assistance with the basic personal tasks of life such as bathing, dressing, personal hygiene, using the toilet, maintaining continence, eating, walking, maintaining mobility, and getting in and out of a bed or chair. Mostly when we think of those who need long-term care we think of people of advanced age, but it is possible to need care when you are younger if you become incapacitated due to a severe illness or tragic accident. The cost of this type of care can be extraordinary. In addition to the cost, if a family member provides some of the care it can be a particularly stressful and time intensive job. Most people explore their options for long-term care insurance when they are in their 50s and early 60s, but it is available to younger people as well, and the premiums are significantly less expensive. We will discuss long-term care and long-term care insurance in detail in the second section of the book.

Life Insurance:

Almost everyone I meet with as a planner is underinsured. You very well may have some coverage through your employer, but it is almost always not enough.

Here are two interesting questions to ask yourself (and you have to be honest!)

1) If life insurance were free, how much would I want?
2) If my spouse or I were killed tragically (think car accident with a drunk driver) how much should my family sue for?

Now compare those numbers to how much life insurance you currently have. Big difference?

Life insurance is so incredibly important and can be relatively cheap. There is no good reason to be uninsured or underinsured. If you have debt and or are responsible for other people financially, you have to have this. It breaks my heart to hear stories of families who are forced to raise their children in relative poverty because one or both of the parents died suddenly.

Sometimes I will ask my clients to close their eyes in the middle of our meeting. We just pause our meeting for a minute. If you have children, please humor me and do the same thing here. Close your eyes for just a minute. Envision your family and your life as it is right now, envision your children right now. Now take a minute to think about and truly envision what life would be like if you, or your spouse, or both of you, weren't here next year. I'll wait.

Ok, now you are probably a bit emotional; hopefully you are, anyway. In that vision, were your spouse and your kids able to stay in the same house? Was there enough money to pay the monthly bills? Were they still able to go on vacations? What about new clothes? What did the holidays look like? Would your children be able to go to college?

These are all very real questions, and not answering them honestly can have serious implications. You see, if you don't have the appropriate amount of life insurance life may be very different for your family if you die suddenly. Even if just one parent dies, if the other parent needs to work multiple jobs just to make ends meet, well in a way, those kids just lost both of their parents, didn't they?

(In infomercial announcer voice) Lucky for you this situation is easily avoidable, for just easy monthly payments of $59.99...I'll get to that later.

When we talk about life insurance, we need to discuss two main points. How much? and what kind? Let's talk about "what kind?" first.

Life insurance comes in two main varieties: term and permanent coverage.

Term Life Insurance

Term, like its name implies, only lasts for a certain period of time. At that point the coverage will lapse, or in some cases you can renew it but the premium will be higher because it will be based on your older age. I don't want to get lost in the weeds, so let's just say the coverage will lapse. Typical terms would be annually renewable, 10 year, 15 year, 20 year, and 30 year. There are other durations of term insurance, but you get the idea.

Think of term insurance as renting life insurance. It is a great temporary solution to a temporary problem. In most cases, the temporary problem is you are young and have a young family that is financially dependent on you and your future earning ability. If you die tragically, big problem. If you have enough term life insurance coverage, big solution. Typically, you can match up the length of term coverage to the length of term need. For example, if you have two children ages three and six, what do we do? Well the 10-year term will expire when the six-year-old is 16 and the three-year-old is 13. That won't cut it. The 15-year term will expire when the kids are eighteen and twenty-one. Eh, that's really kind of cutting it close, huh? Especially nowadays when kids are having a tough time "launching" after school. They are still financially dependent to a degree (sometimes all the degrees!). If these were my clients I would probably recommend either 20-year term, or a combination of 15 and 20-year term. This is just a basic example but you should get the idea.

Another use for term insurance could be to cover a debt. If you have a large debt like a mortgage or student loan where someone else would be responsible for it if you die, please make sure they aren't left holding the bag. Term is a cost effective way to eliminate or highly mitigate the financial risk of unexpected death. If the insured person dies during the term, even on the first day, the death benefit is payable to the beneficiary. The beneficiary will have some options on how to take the money; typical options are lump sum, payments, or annuity options. Life Insurance death benefits are generally income tax free.

Permanent Life Insurance
The other type of life insurance is permanent life insurance. This comes in many flavors with names like Whole Life, Universal Life, Indexed Universal Life, and Variable Universal Life among others. For the sake of brevity, I am not going to go into a several chapter long detailed explanation of the similarities and differences of these products. What you need to know is that permanent life insurance, like its name implies, provides a permanent death benefit so long as the policy is kept in-force. So in theory, even if you die at 100 years old, someone will get the death benefit.

Permanent insurance can build cash value within the policy. The main differences between the types of permanent policies lie in the fee structure and how the cash value grows.

- Whole life—the cash value grows according to a dividend scale that can be adjusted up or down by the insurance company depending on their annual experience with claims.
- Universal life –similar to Whole Life in that the cash value grows according to a stated interest rate that the company can adjust up and down according to market interest rates.
- Variable life—the cash value is invested in variable accounts—stock and bond investments that can fluctuate up and down with the stock and bond markets.
- Indexed Universal life–a bit of a hybrid between universal life and variable universal life. You invest in investments that seek to mirror stock market indices, with certain risk management features included.

Each kind of policy has its pros and cons. A qualified financial advisor or insurance advisor will be able to help match you up to the best type of policy for you and your goals.

Permanent life insurance generally has higher premiums than term insurance in exchange for the cash value build up and the permanent death benefit. So there is certainly a trade-off that must be considered. In a lot of cases, particularly when the family is younger, earnings are lower, and debt is higher, term is more attractive because it does the trick of eliminating the financial risk of an unexpected early death, and is significantly cheaper than permanent coverage thereby fitting into the budget a bit easier.

Usually where educators and their families would utilize permanent life insurance would be if they want to make sure that funds are available to pay their final expenses if they die when they are supposed to die i.e. in their 80s or 90s. Final expenses can include funeral costs, burial costs, medical bills not covered by insurance, final tax bills, final credit card and utility bills, and attorney fees among other expenses.

Sometimes, if the cash flow is ample and the client is attracted to the idea, we will combine a smaller permanent policy to generate the death benefit if death occurs in old age, with a much larger term policy to protect the family while everyone is relatively young. That way, once the kids are out of school or what have you, the term policy will expire as there is no longer a need for that much life insurance. The permanent policy will still be in force to provide funds for final expenses in the case of death in old age.

There are many other beneficial uses for permanent insurance as well. We will cover this in greater detail later in the book, but I thought I would briefly mention them now.

- Some permanent policies offer optional riders, at an additional cost, that can be used to pay for qualified long-term care expenses like nursing homes or custodial or skilled care. Any funds used for these expenses will decrease the policy cash value and death benefit.
- Permanent insurance can guarantee an inheritance for your kids. You could purchase a permanent policy while you are younger, naming your children as beneficiaries. By doing so, you can now spend down all of your other assets in retirement without having to worry about leaving an inheritance for your kids because the insurance will provide the inheritance as the death benefit when you pass. This strategy is becoming increasingly popular as parents are becoming concerned about the financial futures of their children. Their children are facing a world of lower wages, potentially higher taxes, and historically high educational expenses for THEIR children. This strategy provides a way to make sure that your kids have some help financially in the way of an inheritance.

- Permanent coverage is also used for educators, in certain circumstances, in connection with a pension maximization strategy in retirement. We will cover this in detail later.

How much insurance do I need? There are a number of ways to determine this. One way is the "if I die I want all the debt paid off" approach. I am not a big fan of that approach because it potentially leaves the surviving family with an income need. I prefer to reverse engineer the income need and the capital needs to find out what your family will need from you posthumously. What I mean by capital needs is how much the family would need for lump sum expenses such as college for the kids and to pay off the mortgage and car notes and other large debts.

This is where we start:

First, add up all of the household investments and savings such as retirement accounts (IRA's, 401(k)'s, 403(b)'s, etc.), stocks, bonds, mutual funds and savings accounts. Then from that sum subtract capital expenditures like college for the kids, paying off the house, paying off student loans, paying off car loans and expenses related to death like the funeral, burial expenses, possible medical bills, stuff like that. Now you have a number, quite possibly a significant negative number. That number represents the amount of insurance coverage we need just to make sure those expenses are covered.

Now we need to see how much our monthly income is and how much our projected new monthly expenses are. Income sources can be the salary of a surviving spouse, Social Security income, potentially pension income from the deceased spouse. Monthly expenses will be very much like what they used to be except your family won't be paying a mortgage or student loans or car payments anymore. Your family will still need to pay utilities, insurance premiums, put gas in the car, feed and clothe themselves, household maintenance, vacations and so forth.

If there is a monthly deficit after subtracting the expenses from income, we will need more life insurance to bridge that gap on a monthly basis.

There is no cookie cutter way to say how much insurance you need. You need to have a very real conversation with your advisor about what you would want for your family if you were to die early. Everybody's situation is different and varies depending on income, savings, investments, amount of debt, number of children, etc.

That being said, a $1,000,000 20-year level term policy for a 35-year-old male in good health generally might be around $60 in premium per month. Women are usually a little cheaper due to longer life expectancies. Keep in mind that each company has its own underwriting guidelines. We are using age 35 just as an example. If you are younger, the premium will be less, if you are older it will be more. I would argue that in MOST cases this should be enough to keep the family from financial despair if a parent were to pass away unexpectedly. So, again, roughly estimate that for about $100 per month both spouses might be able to acquire an adequate amount of coverage to help save the family from financial failure. When you think about it this way, you can see what I mean when I say there is no excuse not to have the appropriate amount of life insurance. Who wouldn't spend $100 per month to help ensure the safety of their family?

Property and Casualty Insurances:

These will mostly be made up of homeowners or renters insurance, auto insurance, and maybe an umbrella policy. I am not going to spend a lot of time going into detail about the different types of policies available and how much coverage you should have. A good property and casualty agent can certainly be of assistance to you here. However, the reason we mention these insurances is to point out how important they are to your financial plan.

If you have a mortgage on your house, chances are you have home-owner's insurance. It is usually a necessary part of getting a mortgage. If you own your home outright, and choose not to carry coverage; well, that's your prerogative. However, if the house burns down or some other catastrophic disaster occurs, you've got a big problem on your hands. Most people reading this book have homeowners insurance if they own their home. However, again, please meet with your property and casualty agent and make sure you understand what is covered and what isn't. You may be surprised at what you are still exposed to, and also how little extra in premium it might cost to shore up those exposed risks. If you currently rent your house or apartment, get some cheap renters insurance just to make sure you don't lose some or all of your belongings in the event of a fire or burglary, or some other fun kind of event.

If you do not have auto insurance and you wreck somebody's expensive car and possibly put them in the hospital, say goodbye to your savings and investments because you are getting sued, my friend. Dress nice for court. In reality, I haven't had a client who did not have auto insurance, so you too probably have coverage. It is, however, probably worth taking an hour or so to meet with your agent just to make sure you understand how much and what type of coverage you have. It is better to make sure you are properly covered now than after an accident. Oh yeah, by the way, like most things in life, cheaper does not always equal better. If one policy is much cheaper than another, there is probably a reason such as less coverage, etc.

Generally speaking, an umbrella policy is a pretty smart coverage to have. It is inexpensive, and like an umbrella covers you above and beyond what your homeowners and auto policies cover. Typical uses for this policy would be when your friend slips on the ice outside your house and decides they would rather sue you for a million dollars than continue to be your friend. It happens. I would also say it would be a smart coverage if you have a pool at your house. You can probably figure that one out.

Emergency Fund

This is nothing complicated or sexy. A savings account with money in it. Generally speaking, six months of living expenses is about right. But as you'll see the proper amount can depend on a lot of variables. Some of these variables are the following:

1) Job security. If you and your spouse (if married) have very secure employment, you can generally get away with a smaller emergency fund.

2) Credit availability. If you are more established and have a sizable credit line open, like a home equity line of credit or even credit cards in a pinch, this can allow you to have a smaller emergency fund. By the way, I am in no way recommending that you run up your credit cards and get caught in that trap, but if you need a little bit of short term credit, it's not the end of the world.

3) Large investment accounts. If you have substantial investment accounts, you may be able to have a smaller emergency fund because you could tap your investments if push came to shove.

4) Willing and capable family. Both parts of "willing" and "capable" are crucial. If you have family that are well to do and have mentioned that they would be willing to help if you get in a jam, then you may be able to get away with a smaller emergency fund.

5) Comfort level. Some people just are not comfortable with less than six months living expenses in saving—no arguments here.

Now, the reverse holds true as well. If you do not have a very secure job, or your spouse does not have a secure job, you very well might want to have more than six months of expenses in your emergency fund. If you do not have access to lines of credit, or have poor credit you might want to have a larger emergency fund. And if you do not really have much saved in investment accounts, I would suggest that you work on building that emergency fund first.

So sound insurance coverage and a robust, emergency savings account completes the base of the pyramid. Really exciting stuff, huh? But now you know that if somebody asks your opinion on what is the most important part of your financial plan, it's not your 403(b) or Roth IRA, or even your super cool private equity or hedge fund. It's your boring insurances and cash.

Chapter 2 Points to Remember

- The most important parts of your financial plan are your insurances and an emergency fund. Your main insurances are health, disability income (both short and long term), long-term care, life, homeowners/renters, auto, and possibly an umbrella policy
- You probably have health insurance through your employer, but if you have a choice of coverage, you may choose to pay a higher premium for a more comprehensive plan if you have health concerns, or you may choose to pay a smaller premium for less comprehensive coverage if you are young and in good health. Remember, if you have kids, they seem to always be at the doctor's office, particularly when they are young.
- There is a good chance you have short-term disability income coverage through your employer. Ask someone in your human resources department to give you the details of that coverage. Find out if you have long-term disability income coverage. If not, acquire it. If you are married, what are your spouse's benefits?
- Life insurance generally comes in term and permanent varieties. Term is usually a lot cheaper than permanent but will most likely expire worthless at the end of the term. However, this is much better than the alternative, right? Make sure that you have the appropriate amount of coverage, and at the very least, cover yourself with term. If you have additional funds, consider making a portion of your coverage permanent to pay for final expenses if you die when you are "supposed" to die. Free life insurance calculators can be found at www.educatedwealthstrategies.com.
- Spend a little time with your property and casualty agent understanding what all of your policies cover. Are you comfortable with those limits? Most times umbrella policies are a

smart coverage plan, and they are cheap. People like to sue other people. Protect yourself.

- A good starting place for an emergency fund is about six months of living expenses. Adjust up or down for your personal situation. Do not try to get cute with this account: a savings account or money market account will do just fine.

Do I need LTD
w/ PSERS?

CHAPTER 3

RETIREMENT ACCUMULATION PLANNING

THE FINANCIAL PLANNING PYRAMID
(RETIREMENT)

A fter you have the base of your pyramid set up properly with your insurances and an emergency fund you can move on to the next part of your financial plan. This will take the lion's share of your saving and investing funds. I find that the easiest way to plan for retirement income is to start with the end in mind. That is to say, let's figure out what you expect your monthly recurring expenses to be in retirement and how much of an income you will need to cover your expenses. You will also need to account for other expenses in retirement such as out of pocket healthcare costs, possible long-term care or skilled care, possible financial responsibility for your aging parents and/or your adult children who haven't quite yet found their feet. Also, it is interesting to note that quite a large number of people end up retiring before they planned to retire due to health concerns, health concerns of a loved one, job downsizing, job buyouts, etc.

Once we have an idea of what our expenses will be then we can work backwards to figure out how much you need to save each year to generate an income stream that is adequate. We will cover this in more detail in the second part of the book. For now, we will focus mainly on how to accumulate funds. You should have several sources of retirement income.

The main sources of income for most educators are their pension and Social Security. These days pensions can look very different depending on your state and also your employer. If you work for a public school you probably have a defined benefit pension, although these are coming under attack from state governments. If you work in higher education, you may have a defined benefit plan, or a defined contribution plan. If you work in private or parochial schools, you may have either of these as well, although it is less common to have a defined benefit plan in the private school arena.

Defined Benefit Pension
This is what most people think of when they think of a pension. When you retire, you will receive a guaranteed income stream for the rest

of your life. If you pick a survivorship option, your survivor (think spouse) will also receive some income for the rest of their life if you happen to die first. These types of plans instill a sense of security knowing that you will have basically a salary in retirement.

The benefit that you will get in retirement is based on a formula. These formulas are different for each pension system and some have actually changed in recent years, but a good example for illustrative purposes is:

(2.5% X the average of your 3 highest salaries X the # of years of service)

When you know how the formula works, it is easy to figure out what your benefit will be. For example, let's say the average of your three highest salaries is $80,000 and you have 30 years of service. We take 2.5% x $80,000 x 30= $60,000. So in this case you would get $60,000 each year in retirement.

In most cases, these plans do not offer cost of living adjustments (COLA) but it is worth looking into. A cost of living adjustment (COLA) is a feature which gives you a raise each year based on inflation. We will assume throughout this book that defined benefit plans do not have a COLA.

Defined benefit plans have come under fire in the last several years for number of reasons. First, they are expensive to fund and administer. Second, they are risky for the employer. Basically, with a defined benefit pension, the employer or state is guaranteeing you and potentially your survivor an income for the rest of your lives. They must make several assumptions when determining funding levels for the plan. They need to assume how long the retirees will live and collect income, how long will their survivors collect income, what interest rate will the general fund enjoy over the years, what amount of contributions will come in from the participants, etc. If they are incorrect about any of these issues, the pension fund can become underfunded. This is the issue that most states are dealing with regarding their public pension funds. Most of them are underfunded and requiring more funding from the school districts or states, which are already cash strapped.

I just wanted to give you that bit of background so you can better understand the current pension environment. Some states have changed their pension plans, and many others have proposals or plans to alter the structure of their pension plans as well. With that in mind, you may want to plan on saving a bit more for retirement than you normally would to protect yourself if your pension plan changes (hint: it probably won't change for the better).

Employer-Sponsored Defined Contribution Plans

For most of you this will be a 403(b) plan. A 403(b) plan is the non-profit sector's version of a 401(k) plan. That being said, it is possible for some educators outside of the public school system (private) to have a 401(k) instead of a 403(b). It would function similarly to what I am about to describe.

A 403(b) can be funded with both employee and employer money. Employee money is deposited via payroll deduction. The maximum that can be contributed in 2015 is the lesser of 100% of compensation or $18,000 for those under 50 years old. For those 50 and older, they can contribute an additional $6,000 as a catch-up contribution for a total of $24,000. These numbers tend to increase each year, so it is always a good idea to double check the maximum limits for the tax year with your advisor, HR department at school, or www.irs.gov. It is also important to understand that these are just the limits of what YOU can contribute to your plans. The limits are much higher when you take employer contributions into consideration.

While there are certainly exceptions to this, I would say that generally if your employer provides a defined benefit pension plan, you will probably not have employer money deposited into your 403(b), but you can and should still contribute your own money. If you are in higher education, private school, or are not part of a defined benefit plan, your employer may contribute money to a 403(b) or 401(k) for you, and again, you can contribute your own money. Sometimes we also see cases where certain bargaining groups such as administrators receive employer funds into their 403(b)s.

There is yet another type of defined contribution plan available for public school employees. It is the 457(b) deferred compensation plan. This is a retirement plan for governmental employees. Public schools are unique in that they are governmental non-profit entities. Therefore, they can sponsor both 403(b) and 457(b) plans. 457(b) plans are a bit different from 403(b) and 401(k) plans in that they are technically deferred compensation plans and not elective deferral retirement plans. 457(b) plans have contribution limits similar to 403(b) and 401(k).

There are some slight differences between the plans concerning when you can access your money. With 403(b) and 401(k) plans you generally cannot withdraw funds without IRS penalties before the age of 59.5 **OR** age 55 and severed from service with your employer. The main exception to this rule would be accessing your money through a loan in which you need to pay yourself back within a certain number of years.

With the 457(b) plan, there is no age requirement, just a severance from service requirement (www.IRS.gov). So you could be 40 years old and sever service from your employer and have access to the funds without penalty; although the funds would still be subject to income tax. If you think about this for a minute, it makes sense. 457(b) plans are what are used by police officers and other municipal employees. Police officers generally retire after about 20 to 30 years on the job. So if they started working at 22 they would only be 42 to 52 years old at retirement. With their 457(b) they could access their money. So can a public school teacher or administrator.

I can think of at least three scenarios where a 457(b) could come in handy. First, for the teacher or administrator who wants to max out contributions to both a 403(b) and a 457(b); this would allow them to essentially double up their contributions. Second, for an administrator who plans on switching employers for career advancement. Each time they change employers, their old 457(b) is available to them to access. Third, for teachers who may know that they are going to leave teaching for a number of years, or possibly forever, to raise a family this would give them access to the funds without penalty.

To Roth or not to Roth

Traditionally speaking, 403(b), 401(k) and 457(b) plans are funded with pre-tax dollars. Now in many plans you have the option to contribute in pre-tax OR Roth dollars. Let's discuss how the traditional pre-tax method works. You contribute via payroll deduction, and funds are sent to your account pre-tax. This means that you get a tax deduction in the current year for whatever your annual contribution is. For example, if your salary is $50,000 and you contribute $5000 over the course of the year, you will only show taxable income of $45,000. Once the money goes into the account it grows tax deferred until you withdraw money in retirement. At that point it will be taxed as ordinary income just like your salary is taxed now.

Roth contributions work in the opposite way. The contributions are taxed before they go into your account, but once they are in the account they accumulate tax free and come out tax free.

So which is the better way to contribute? It depends on your personal situation. Here are a couple things to consider. The country has a tremendous amount of debt at this point, and the current tax environment is relatively low. That could indicate that taxes will be going up in the future. If that is the case, it's a pretty strong argument for Roth contributions because it would be better to pay taxes now at a lower rate and take distributions tax free (when taxes are higher). However, you will live for many years in retirement and probably see many different tax scenarios in retirement. Also, while you are accumulating for retirement you will see many different tax environments. So that makes the decision a bit less clear, right? Hmm, ok, next part.

If you have a defined benefit pension plan like most public school teachers, this is funded with pre-tax dollars. It will be taxable to you when you collect your pension in retirement. If your spouse has a pension, that too will most likely be taxable. So the advice that I give to most of my clients is to save mostly in Roth dollars if you already have a pension plan that is pre-tax. This is in an effort to provide tax diversification in retirement.

What I mean by tax diversification is that we ultimately want to have some accounts that will be taxable when we withdraw and some accounts that will be tax free when we withdraw. This will provide us with flexibility from a taxation perspective. If we enter a period of time in retirement when tax rates increase substantially, we can draw more from our tax-free accounts. If we enter a period of time when tax rates decrease substantially, we can hit our pre-tax accounts harder. We can also blend our income from both sources, therefore keeping our overall taxable income lower. According to the current tax code, our income is taxed at marginal tax rates. That means that the more income we show, the higher our tax bracket becomes.

Here is an example of what I mean using two scenarios. This example is EXTREMELY simplified to better explain the concept. We will assume that we want a $100,000 income in retirement. Let's also assume that the effective tax rate on a $100,000 income is 25%; and the effective tax rate on a $50,000 income is 10% (lower income so lower tax rate, right?).

Scenario 1: In this scenario we take all $100,000 out of pre-tax accounts. We would show $100,000 of income. We would pay $25,000 in taxes and clear $75,000 after taxes.

Scenario 2: In this scenario we take $50,000 from our pre-tax accounts and $50,000 from our Roth accounts for a total of $100,000. We would only show income of $50,000 from the pre-tax account. The Roth money comes out tax free. So we would only owe $5,000 in taxes from the $50,000 distribution of the pre-tax account ($50,000x10%). In total, we would have our $100,000 income, but only pay $5,000 in total taxes. We clear $95,000 after taxes.

Who prefers scenario 1? That's what I thought.

We have to be honest with ourselves; we have no idea what the tax environment will look like in 5, 10, 30 years. We can make our best guesses, but we really have no idea. If you believe anybody on TV who says they know, give me a call because I have some magic beans I want to sell you.

We can hedge our tax exposure simply by saving in both Roth and pre-tax accounts. If you do not have a defined benefit pension, or sizable pre-tax account balances in 403(b), 401(k), or 457(b) accounts, you may simply want to save 50/50 in both Roth and pre-tax plans. Again, this is more sophisticated planning and you need to take into account your own personal situation and that of your spouse. A good advisor can bring value to you here.

To recap and to clarify as I have been throwing around a lot of numbers and letters; here are your basic choices when it comes to Employer- Sponsored Defined Contribution plans:

403(b): Public schools; some private schools, some higher education.
457(b): Public schools; governmental entities.
401(k): Some private schools; for-profit companies.

IRA- Individual Retirement Account

Outside of your employer-sponsored options, you may able to contribute to IRAs as well. IRAs come in both traditional pre-tax and Roth versions. The contribution limits are much lower than 403(b), 457(b) and 401(k), but they can provide more investment flexibility. With employer-sponsored plans you are generally limited in your investment choices. In an IRA you have thousands of different investment options available. This can be a great benefit, but can also hurt you if you choose poor investments. Another limitation in IRAs has to do with your income. If you make too much money you may not be able to deduct your contributions to a traditional IRA and you may not be able to contribute at all to a Roth IRA.

However, what tends to work out well for a lot of educators is to contribute to a 403(b) or 457(b) and also contribute to a Roth IRA. A Roth IRA has the same tax treatment as Roth 403(b) but also has some added flexibility. Part of that added flexibility is in the funding options. With a 403(b) or 457(b) you can only fund via payroll deduction and all funding must be completed by the end of the year. With an IRA, both traditional pre-tax as well as Roth, you can write checks to your account at your convenience and you also have until April 15th of the following year to make your contributions for the previous year. This comes in handy if you had a really good idea (wink, wink, nod, nod) of using your tax refund as a contribution to your Roth IRA. As I said, it isn't the right prescription for everyone, but in a lot of situations funding a 403(b), either in pretax or Roth dollars, and a Roth IRA concurrently is hard to argue with.

These basically cover the bases of common retirement accounts available and utilized by teachers. There are some other accounts available if you own a business outside of school, or have a part-time job in the summer, but in an effort to keep this book reasonably easy to follow I will not address these plans here.

Social Security

In the majority of states, teachers contribute to, and are covered by Social Security. There are a number of states in which this is not the case, though. If you are not sure you should double check with your human resources department (HR) or business office, or you can refer to your paystub to see if you are having deductions for Social Security. Lastly, you can always go to www.socialsecurity.gov and set up your account online to view your account details.

It is critically important to determine whether you and your spouse will be covered by Social Security in retirement. It will provide a good chunk of income for your life and it also has a cost of living adjustment (COLA). This is a very powerful feature and is not to be taken lightly. Now I hear you saying "But Eric, Social Security is broke, there's no way it's going to be there for me!" There are certainly a fair share of people who share this sentiment, but I would say that we will probably all get Social Security (assuming you are covered under Social Security in the first place). Social Security has gone through changes and amendments in the past, and it will probably need to go through changes in the future. Some of these changes may take the shape of higher Social Security taxes, raising the wage base, slightly decreasing the benefit or decreasing the COLA, raising the retirement age, or a combination of some or all of these moving parts. However, and this is just my opinion, but I think it reflects common sense; if Social Security goes bankrupt there will be the equivalent of another Civil War in this country. Could you imagine for a minute what would happen if all of the millions upon millions of citizens who contributed to Social Security for their whole working lives were told that they will get nothing out of it? I can imagine such a change causing riots in the streets and a complete collapse of government. No President and Congress will ever let that happen, but they (as usual) will probably wait until the last minute to solve systemic problems. Anyway, I could be wrong but I would rather bet on small changes made to the current system over the alternative.

Currently there are two big issues that can affect those who are employees of the federal, state, or local governments and are NOT covered by Social Security. If you fit into this group, this is very important for you to know and understand.

GPO (Government Pension Offset): The GPO will reduce or possibly eliminate your Social Security spousal or survivor benefits. The amount of the benefit reduction is equal to two-thirds of your public pension. Normally, if your spouse who was covered under Social Security either retired or passed away, you would be eligible for full spousal or survivor benefits. The GPO reduces or eliminates these benefits. (www.nea.org)

WEP (Windfall Elimination Provision): The WEP can affect you if you:

1) Work or have worked as a public employee NOT covered by Social Security; and,
2) You have also worked or will work in jobs that ARE covered by Social Security.

For example, if you had a previous career in the private sector where you were covered under Social Security, or are currently working part-time or during the summer at a job that is covered by Social Security, your benefits can be significantly reduced. Another example would be if you previously worked for a public school that was covered by Social Security and then later worked for a public school that was not covered under Social Security. (www.nea.org)

Again, it is important to understand that the GPO and WEP only come into play if you have worked or will work as a public employee NOT covered by Social Security.

Other Investments That Can Be Used for Retirement Income

- Rental property or Investment Real Estate
- Stocks, Bonds, Mutual Funds, Exchange Traded Funds, Master Limited Partnerships (MLP's), alternative investments, etc.
- Annuities

We will discuss these in more detail in in the second section of the book.

How Much Do I Need to Save for Retirement?

This is the million-dollar question –sorry, pun intended- I couldn't help it. The answer to this question depends on the answers to many other questions. When do you want to retire? When is your spouse planning to retire? How much does he/she have saved? How much is he/she currently saving? How are your retirement assets invested; and what is the expected rate of return? Are either of you covered under pension plans? How about Social Security? Will the mortgage be paid off before you retire? What will your monthly bills look like at that time? What are your plans in retirement? Do you want to travel; if so, are we talking RV travelling the US or touring the French Riviera on your private yacht? You get the idea. In order to get a good idea of how much you need to save for retirement, we need to have a very clear picture of what kind of lifestyle you want to live, and for how long.

I really don't like to use generalizations, especially with something so important, but if you were to save 15% of your income from the time you started working until you retire and you have reasonable expectations in retirement, you should be in good shape. If you aren't saving the appropriate amount (most people), try your best to adjust your lifestyle to free up the funds to save more. Usually you will find that there is fat in the budget that can be trimmed. If you do not have enough saved for retirement when you reach that age, you have two options 1) work longer, or 2) die earlier. I'd rather not be faced with either, right? A good advisor can help you determine how much you need to save to accomplish your goals in retirement.

Going back to all of those questions that I rattled off, there is one that seems innocuous but is very important. "How are your retirement assets invested, and what is the expected rate of return?"

"I don't know, I just kinda picked some different mutual funds and (voice trails off)..." What I've seen over the years is that teachers are generally pretty conservative people when it comes to money. They work really hard for it and they don't want to lose it. What that tends to lead to is portfolios that are heavily skewed to bonds, cash, and guaranteed interest accounts for "safety." They don't realize that what they don't know is killing them.

In working with so many teachers I've come to understand that a lot of teachers don't fully understand the difference between stocks and bonds and don't fully understand what a mutual fund is. Let's take a minute to go over these basics so we have a good foundation of knowledge for the rest of the book.

Stocks. Stocks represent ownership in a company. When you buy a share of General Electric stock you are a very small, partial owner of GE. When the company does well, more people want to be owners of the company and that drives up the demand and, therefore the price, of the stock. The company is worth more, so your shares of stock are worth more. If you sell them, you would make a profit. However, if the company does not do well, people would no longer be interested in owning shares, therefore driving the price of the stock down. If you sell your shares now you would lose money. As a shareholder, you can be entitled to dividends from the company as well. Because stocks represent ownership or equity in a particular company, they are sometimes referred to as equities. When somebody refers to the "equity portion" of their portfolio, you now know that they are talking about the part of their portfolio that is stock based.

Bonds. Bonds represent debt. They are primarily issued by private and public companies, municipalities, states, the federal government, and governments of other countries. When an entity needs to raise money, they may consider issuing bonds to raise the capital. In basic terms, they are a loan. They pay an interest rate called a coupon and at the end of the loan term, you are repaid your money. You as an investor do not own any equity in a company if you buy their bonds. You are simply lending the company money in exchange for promised interest payments and the eventual return of your money. Bonds are referred to as debt, or fixed income. So now when somebody is talking about the fixed income portion of their portfolio, you know that they are probably talking about bonds.

Mutual Funds. Mutual funds were created to give average investors with modest amounts of money access to stocks and bonds in diversified portfolios. Essentially a mutual fund is a collection of stocks and/or bonds. The creation of mutual funds was an appealing idea to many people because now with a small amount of money one could own stocks or bonds from many different companies instead of just one or two. This provided diversification and greatly reduced the chance that one could lose everything they had simply by one company going bankrupt.

There are a tremendous number of mutual funds available now. Some are stock based, some are bond based, some are a combination of the two. Some focus on large companies, some on small companies, some international. Some are actively managed; some are passively managed. I am not going to go into great detail about all the different types of mutual funds. What I want you to understand is that they are collections of stocks and/or bonds created to provide diversification.

The lawyers tell me that I have to include the following, so here it goes: *Mutual funds are sold by prospectus. The prospectus contains information on the funds, including investment objectives, risks, charges and expenses. You should obtain and read the prospectus and consider this information carefully before investing or sending money.*

Ok, moving along...

Now that we have a basic understanding of the differences between stocks and bonds, let's talk about their long-term rates of return.

From 1926-2012, US large company stocks have returned roughly 10% annualized. US Long-Term Government Bonds have returned about 6% and Cash (T-bills, savings accounts, etc.) has returned about 3.5%. I had a professor in college tell me something that I thought was funny and very true. He said "Statistics are like bikinis; what they show is interesting, but what they hide is critical." So, applying that understanding to the above statistics, we need to understand that inflation has been in the ballpark of 3% annually on average. So in inflation-adjusted or "real" terms, stocks have returned about 7%, bonds about 3% and cash roughly 0.5%. (Morningstar)

Asset Class	Nominal Rate of Return	Inflation Adjusted Rate of Return
US Large Company Stocks	10%	7%
US Long Term Gov't Bonds	6%	3%
Cash	3.5%	0.5%
Inflation	3%	N/A

The difference between 7% and 3% (stocks vs bonds) may not seem like a big deal on the surface, but over time the difference can be substantial.

In the spirit of keeping this book basic, we will use the rule of 72 to figure out the future growth of a hypothetical investment. The rule of 72 is a quick and dirty way to figure out compound interest growth. What you do is divide the interest rate you assume to get into 72 and the result will be roughly how many years it will take your money to double. For example, if we use a 10% interest rate it will take roughly 7.2 years for the money to double (72/10=7.2). If we use a 7% interest rate it will take about 10.28 years for the money to double (72/7=10.28). Again, let's just round these numbers off to keep from getting bogged down.

So assuming a 7% interest rate it would have taken about 10 years for our money to double. Let's assume we started with $10,000 and had 40 years for the money to accumulate until we needed to spend it. This is four "doublings." $10,000 would have doubled to $20,000; then doubled to $40,000, then doubled to $80,000, then doubled to $160,000. That is pretty incredible! Bear in mind that this is a hypothetical illustration showing a 7% average return over 40 years. Just to paint a picture for you.

Now, let's use roughly a 3% interest rate. This means that roughly every 24 years the money would double (72/3). If we had 40 years to grow the money it would experience just under two doublings. So

$10,000 would have turned into $20,000, and then $20,000 would have turned into slightly less than $40,000, say $37,000ish. Again, this is a hypothetical situation assuming a 3% average return over 40 years.

Demonstrating the historical growth of cash is easy. A 0.5% real rate of return (3.5%-3%=0.5%) means that you get basically no real growth over time. The $10,000 would have grown to just slightly more than $12,000. Super! Pass the caviar!

So to compare the three hypothetical rates of return after 40 years:

- 7%: $160,000
- 3%: $37,000
- 0.5%: $12,000

That is a very big cost for "safety." Of course the gap just widens and widens over time. If you gave the portfolio another 10 years to grow the 7% return would have doubled again to $320,000, the 3% return would modestly grow and the 0.5% return would be worth- wait for it- less than $13,000. It is important to note that past performance is not guaranteed in the future.

In all of these examples I used inflation-adjusted figures; I think this is important. When you see advertisements or read in magazines something along the lines of "How to Save $1,000,000 Easily," a lot of times they are using nominal rates of return, not inflation-adjusted rates. That's all well and good, but remember what I said about statistics and bikinis: one million dollars 30 years from now will not be worth anywhere near what one million dollars is worth today, as one million dollars today is not worth anything near what it was 30 years ago. I think it is most helpful to use inflation-adjusted figures so you get a clear picture of what your wealth will be "worth" in the future.

A couple of notes and disclosure about all this. First, I fully admit these are rough "ballpark" numbers. Also, one can manipulate the data to show slightly higher or lower rates of return for stocks, bonds, cash, and inflation over time simply by using data from different time periods. You can, and should work with your advisor or determine on your own what long term growth rate you want to use in your planning. Also, I demonstrated the rule of 72 simply to show you how to figure out compound interest growth in your head. It is not exact. You can certainly use an online retirement calculator to help you figure out exactly what the accounts might grow to.

Throughout these calculations and examples of growth rates, I hope that you picked up on a VERY IMPORTANT issue. The sooner you get started saving the better! You will have much more time for the money to compound and it will make a HUGE difference on the end value of your portfolio. Do not wait until "later" to start saving for retirement. There will always be an excuse or a reason why "now" is not a good time to save. The most important years to save are in your early 20s because that money will participate in many more years of compounding.

As you can see, there are many different ways to save for retirement. You can participate in any combination of 403(b), 457(b), IRA, Roth IRA, or brokerage accounts (discussed later); however, it is very important to make sure that your asset allocation is appropriate for your individual goals and needs for long term growth.

Another often overlooked aspect is the fee structure of the accounts you use. Fees can erode returns over time. Each account will have a different fee structure and it's important that you understand it. We will now briefly go over what you can expect to find in the different types of accounts you will encounter.

403(b) and 457(b) plans:
These accounts are typically funded either by variable annuities or mutual funds. We will cover variable annuities first:

A variable annuity is issued by an insurance company but it is not life insurance. In a typical variable annuity based 403(b) or 457(b) the product will offer a number of stock and bond based funds called sub-accounts or variable investment options. They look and smell just like mutual funds, but they are only available through the variable annuity. They fluctuate with the market just like mutual funds. They range from very aggressive to very conservative. Some variable annuities only offer a handful of sub-accounts and some offer upwards of 100. Variable annuities typically also offer a Guaranteed Interest Account or Fixed account. This account typically pays a better interest rate than one can find at the local bank and can be attractive for some people nearing or currently in retirement. You can generally spread out your investments among any number of sub-accounts and/or the fixed account. You can usually make transfers between the different accounts without incurring any trading fees. When it comes time to start making withdrawals from the account in retirement, you usually will have several options —including periodic withdrawals whenever you need money, systematic withdrawals on a monthly or quarterly basis, or you can choose to annuitize some or all of your account balance. "Annuitizing" is when you give an insurance company a sum of money in exchange for a guaranteed income stream for the rest of your life.

Once again, the lawyers say I should put in some fine print. Pretend I am saying this very fast—like at the end of a TV pharmaceutical commercial where they list all the side effects!

Variable deferred annuities are long-term financial products designed for retirement purposes. In essence, annuities are contractual agreements in which payment(s) are made to an insurance company, which agrees to pay out an income or a lump sum amount at a later date. There are contract limitations and fees and charges associated with annuities, which include, but are not limited to, mortality and expense risk charges, sales and surrender charges, administrative fees, and charges for optional benefits. A financial professional can provide cost information and complete details.

All guarantees are backed by the claims paying ability of the issuing company.

Many Variable Annuities offer optional riders, such as guaranteed benefits, that are available, at an additional cost, and are subject to certain restrictions and limitations.

Please consider the investment objectives, charges, risks, and expenses carefully before purchasing a variable annuity. For a prospectus containing this and other information, please contact a financial professional. Read it carefully before you invest or send money.

Whew, ok I'm done!

Back to the book.

The fee structure of a variable annuity is usually comprised of an annual mortality and expense charge (M&E charge) and the internal cost of the variable investment options chosen.

1) M&E charge: This can range greatly from under 1% to around 2% with the average being 1.25%. (www.sec.gov) This fee is usually levied on the variable investment options in the account; if there is a guaranteed interest option it is generally not applied to any dollars invested there.
2) Cost of the Variable Investment Options: These can range as well from less than half a percent to over 1%. They can vary greatly by different investment and insurance companies. There are typically no fees in the Guaranteed Interest Account (fixed account.)
3) Surrender Charge: Charge that could be levied if you liquidate your account before a certain period of time has elapsed

(surrender period). These periods and charges can vary greatly.

Now, we all need to understand that there are literally hundreds if not thousands of variable annuities in existence with all different fee structures. To paint them all with the same brush would be inaccurate and unfair. I will say most people will probably end up paying somewhere around 1.5% annually in fees with a variable annuity funded 403(b) or 457(b). It could be lower or higher based on the company used, investments chosen, and overall allocation, but if I was forced to pick a number this is probably a reasonably accurate figure.

Outside of 403(b) and 457(b) plans there are many more types of variable annuities available with differing bells and whistles, guarantees, and fees. I could write another book on all of these products, but it is beyond the scope of this project (note: I can think of about a million things I would rather do than write a book about variable annuities!)

Some 403(b) and 457(b) plans are funded by mutual funds. As previously mentioned, mutual funds are essentially a collection of different stocks and/or bonds. They help to provide diversification in a portfolio. For example, you could own shares of individual stocks like IBM. If you own IBM and it goes bankrupt, you could lose everything. Alternatively, you could buy shares of the S&P 500 index mutual fund. Now instead of just owning IBM, you own a tiny piece of IBM and tiny pieces of the other 499 largest companies in the US. If IBM goes bankrupt, you don't lose everything. You own it, but you also own the other 499 companies as well. When you have a portfolio of several mutual funds you can become very diversified among thousands of different companies of all different sizes, industries, and geographic locations.

The fee structures of these plans are typically similar to this:

1) Annual operating & management expenses: all mutual funds have these. They can range from around .2% for a low cost

index fund, to over 2% for some actively managed funds. (www.ICIFactbook.org)

2) Sales Charges (Loads): These are fees that are applied to your investments at the time that money is being invested. They can start off around 5-6% (www.ICIFactbook.org) but they get lower as your invest more money with the same fund family. This is called hitting breakpoints. The first breakpoint is usually around $25,000.

3) Redemption Charges: These are fees that could apply if you sell your funds before a certain period of time has elapsed.

You should read the mutual fund's prospectus for a complete run down of the fees that the fund charges.

It is difficult to forecast how much you would pay in fees with a mutual fund based 403(b) or 457(b), as it largely depends on whether you are investing in stock or bond funds, which fund family you are investing in, which share class you are buying, whether you are getting breakpoints and discounts on your sales charges, or whether you are investing in a no-load, low fee account.

Some people, especially on internet forums, will argue to death about whether variable annuity or mutual fund 403(b)'s and 457(b)'s are better, which one is cheaper, and so on and so forth. I highly recommend working with a competent advisor who understands both options so you can make an informed decision about which option appeals to you most. Generally speaking, variable annuities may be seen as more attractive for those who find value in guarantees. Mutual fund based accounts may be seen as more attractive by those simply seeking long-term investment growth without guarantees.

It is important to note that you may have a choice among several 403(b) or 457(b) providers at your employer. I have seen school districts offer over 20 options of "approved" providers. I have also seen employers offer only one provider. If the latter is the case, then obviously you won't have a choice between mutual fund or variable annuity—you get what you get.

Roth IRAs and Traditional IRAs. You can practically invest in anything with few exceptions in these accounts. Individual stocks and bonds, mutual funds, exchange traded funds, variable and fixed annuities, real estate, even artwork and classic cars in some cases. In my experience, most people fund their IRAs with mutual funds and possibly some individual stocks. As Exchange Traded Funds (ETF's) become more popular I predict we will see more and more of these as well. The fee structure can vary greatly in these accounts as well. If the account is funded with no-load funds with very low internal expenses, these accounts can be very cost effective; however, you will get little to no investment advice or assistance managing your account. These types of funds are typically best for do-it-yourselfers who are investment savvy.

Taxable Investment Accounts: I am using these terms as a catch all for investment accounts that are not technically retirement accounts and do not provide any additional tax benefits. These are also known as brokerage accounts or managed accounts. It is important to note that while they are not technically retirement accounts they can certainly be used to accumulate funds for retirement so they bear mentioning in this chapter. The investments that one can buy and hold in these accounts would be similar to those in IRAs and Roth IRAs. You can hold practically anything in these accounts. The benefit of these accounts is that there aren't any age or severance from service restrictions on your withdrawals like you see with retirement plans. However, there are not any tax incentives either. Remember that withdrawals from qualified retirement plans are subject to ordinary income tax after age 59.5 and are subject to an additional 10% penalty for withdrawals made prior to age 59.5. We will go into more detail about taxable accounts in the next chapter.

If you are working with an advisor, your investment accounts (IRA, Roth IRA, and Taxable Investment Accounts) will more than likely be structured in one of three ways and there are pros and cons to each.

1) **Transactional Based Brokerage.** In this arrangement you pay a fee or a commission every time something is bought or sold in your account. If you do not trade often this could be a

pretty cost effective way to go as fees or commissions are only generated when you buy or sell. Remember, if you are buying mutual funds you still have those annual operating and management expenses as well.

2) **Fee-Based Advisory.** In this arrangement there are can be a combination of fees and commissions. The advisor will typically charge a fee for advice or to manage your portfolio. This is usually set up as a percentage of assets under management. It will normally be somewhere around 1%; with slightly higher charges for smaller accounts and typically slightly lower charges for accounts north of several million dollars (www.bankrate.com). Again, if you are investing in mutual funds or similar products, there are the annual operating and management expenses of the funds to consider as well.

3) **Fee-Only Advisory.** In this arrangement, the advisor usually does not make commissions, but rather charges a flat rate to create a financial plan, charges a fee based on a percentage of assets under management, or charges an hourly or monthly rate similar to how an attorney or accountant would charge.

Permanent Life Insurance. Life insurance is an important tool regarding someone's overall plan. The death benefit provided by life insurance can help to provide funds to take care of ongoing costs, final expenses or to provide a legacy to heirs or a charity.

For those with higher incomes, permanent life insurance can also be an attractive addition to your overall accumulation planning. Life insurance should only be purchased to fill the needs for a death benefit. However, if you own permanent life insurance, as you near retirement, the need for the death benefit may be reduced. At this point it may be advantageous to access the policy's cash value through withdrawals and loans. There can be very nice tax benefits regarding the accumulation and distribution of the cash value within a policy. In general, withdrawals from the cash value can be made up to the basis paid, which means the accumulated value of premiums paid to keep the policy in-force. In addition, loans can be taken against the cash value of the policy, and these loans will accrue as loans do. Any withdrawals, loans and interest will decrease the value of both the death benefit and the policy cash value. If structured correctly, the withdrawals and loans can be taken income tax free.

Investment or Rental Real Estate. Some people feel more comfortable with a tangible investment. Something that they can hold and see. For these people, they may feel more comfortable investing in real estate. You can buy properties to eventually sell for profit, or you can buy properties to rent out for income. There are many unique tax implications both favorable and not associated with investment real estate and they are outside the scope of this book. Just be aware that if you decide to go down this road, you should have a mastery of the tax code as pertains to real estate, or preferably hire a CPA or other competent tax advisor to help you. Real estate can make a great addition to your overall portfolio, but make sure you know what you are getting into before you jump in with both feet.

With all of these choices available to you it can be a bit confusing as to how to save for retirement. If you are covered by Social Security you have a leg up on those that do not. Most of you in the public school arena are covered by pensions of some sort while those in higher education may be covered by a pension or a defined contribution plan. The general rule of thumb that I propose is the following:

If your employer offers matching contributions to your 403(b) or 401(k) plan, make sure that you are at least contributing at the level that allows you to get the full match. For example, if your plan provides a dollar for dollar match up to 3% of your compensation, make sure that you are at least contributing 3% to that plan. If you are not, you are leaving free money on the table. If you can contribute in Roth dollars to that plan, I would probably go that route. Then after you max out your match, you can choose to contribute to a Roth IRA until you max that out. Then if you still have more money to save, go back to your 403(b) or other employer sponsored plan and continue to contribute there.

If your situation is such that you will be considering an early retirement (before age 55) Roth IRAs, 457(b) plans, non-retirement investment accounts, and possibly accessing cash value from permanent life insurance would be good options because you can access some or all of your money earlier than 403(b), 401(k), and IRAs will allow.

Basics of Creating Portfolios:
I feel that I should briefly cover and give you a basic understanding of how to create a diversified portfolio. All too many times when I review a "homemade" account that the client thinks is diversified, they are shocked when I reveal to them that it is not well diversified at all. Just because a portfolio contains a lot of different holdings does not mean that it is diversified. I have seen countless portfolios that were thought to be diversified that had five different mutual funds that were all large company domestic funds. These funds basically held 80% of the same stocks!

While we do manage some accounts with individual stocks, I feel that it is in the best interest of the vast majority of the population to use mutual funds and exchange traded funds (ETFs) to create their portfolios. Warren Buffett is one of the most successful investors of all time and is incredibly skilled as a stock picker. You, however, are not Warren Buffett. It takes an incredible amount of time, intelligence, and patience to successfully pick individual stocks year after year. You very well may have the intelligence, but you probably don't have the time or the patience. You almost certainly would be better off using mutual funds and ETFs to create diversity in your portfolio. As was mentioned earlier, if you own stock in a company and the company goes bankrupt, you can lose everything. In order for you to lose everything in a mutual fund like the S&P 500 index fund, you would need 500 large companies in the United States to simultaneously lose their value. If that ever does happen, you will have bigger problems to worry about than your portfolio. It's time to sit on the porch and guard your canned goods.

More fine print here: *You cannot invest directly in an index. Index funds are created and strive to match the movement of the benchmark index.*

In creating a diversified portfolio, you may consider several or all of the following asset classes (in mutual fund or exchange traded fund form):

- Large company US stock
- Mid-Size company US stock
- Small Company US Stock
- Developed International Stock
- Emerging Markets International Stock
- Long Term Bonds
- Intermediate Term Bonds
- Short Term Bonds
- Cash

If you put together a portfolio with exposure to several or all of these asset classes, you will have a well-diversified portfolio and probably have exposure to several thousand companies of all different sizes and industries throughout the world. There are many funds available that focus on these different asset classes. Now, please understand that this is extremely basic. We do not have any commodities or other "alternative investments" listed here, we have not had any discussion about growth or value oriented funds, or the difference between active and passive fund management. We haven't gone over in what proportions to allocate to the different asset classes. Those types of issues are the finer nuances of portfolio construction. Many of them are hotly debated such as active vs. passive management. The point that I wanted to make was that you should have exposure to a variety of asset classes in your overall portfolio. Five funds of large company US stock does not make a diversified portfolio.

At this point you may be asking what the big deal is with diversification. Why does it matter? Diversification serves a number of roles, but in my opinion this is the most important reason.

It helps to smooth out the ups and downs of the market making it psychologically easier to invest for the long term. Stocks fluctuate in value on a daily basis. Some years they are up a lot, in some years they are down. They do not move in lock-step with each other, in fact they can move in opposite directions. For example, if US large companies are not performing well, international stocks may be performing very well and vice versa. This helps to smooth out the roller coaster ride and can be very beneficial in helping investors not to sell their investments out of fear when the market is temporarily down.

Lastly, I thought I would briefly explain Dollar Cost Averaging (DCA). DCA is a strategy where you may be able to buy into investments at a lower average price over time. When you are a participant in your 403(b) or 457(b) plan you are automatically investing the same amount of money into the same investments with every payroll deduction. With the exception of when you take action to increase or decrease your contribution amount, your investment amount is static.

When the share prices of the investments are high, you buy fewer shares. When the share prices are lower, you buy more shares. This allows you to accumulate more shares over time because your average share price is lower. For example, let's say you invest $100 with each paycheck. If the share price of the investment is $20/share, you will buy 5 shares. When it is $19/share you will buy 5.26 shares. When it is $18/share you will buy 5.56 shares, and so on. I am sure you have heard that the way to make money in the stock market is to buy low and sell high. This is an automatic way to buy fewer shares when the price gets higher and to buy more shares when the price is lower. Here is an example:

Payroll Deduction	$ Amount	Price/Share	Number of Shares Purchased
1	$100	$20	5
2	$100	$19	5.26
3	$100	$18	5.55
4	$100	$17	5.88
5	$100	$18	5.55
6	$100	$19	5.26
7	$100	$20	5
	Total: $700		37.5

So based on this chart, we have a total investment of $700 over 7 payroll periods and we ended up with 37.5 shares. If we would have invested all $700 at the beginning when the price per share was $20 we would have only received 35 shares.

In this hypothetical example, because we Dollar Cost Averaged, we ended up getting 2.5 more shares and a lower average cost per share at $18.66 ($700/37.5 shares).

Magic? Nope, just math.

It is important to note that although dollar cost averaging eliminates the guesswork of market timing, it does not guarantee a profit or protect against loss in a declining market. You should consider your financial ability to commit to a dollar cost averaging strategy, particularly in declining markets.

Chapter 3 Points to Remember:

- You may or may not be covered by a defined benefit pension plan. This is the type of plan most people think of when they think of a pension. It will provide a "salary" for the rest of your life and your spouse's life if you choose a survivorship option. These are very expensive and risky for employers/state governments to maintain so they have come under fire recently. It is important for you to know if you are covered by a pension and how the benefit formula works.

- You may or may not be covered under Social Security. You can find out quickly by checking your paystub for a deduction, or you can contact your HR or payroll office to find out for sure. If you are married, you should also check into this for your spouse.

- Social Security and pensions can provide a very large chunk of your retirement income. It is critically important that you understand how much you stand to get from these programs in retirement.

- If you are not covered by a pension or Social Security, you need to save more on your own. Do not wait until it is too late; the earlier you start the better.

- Common retirement accounts are 403(b), 457(b), 401(k), IRAs, and Roth IRAs. To a lesser extent the investments held in taxable accounts like brokerage accounts and managed investment accounts, real estate, and life insurance.

- You will need to save a lot of money for retirement, especially if you plan to retire early. Lots of people end up retiring earlier than planned. If you are looking at a 25-30yr+ retirement this will require a lot of income and inflation will erode your purchasing power each year.

- How you have your money invested is very important. Whether you are using variable annuities, mutual funds, exchange traded funds, or individual stocks and bonds you need to understand the power of compound interest for two reasons. First, the sooner you get started the better (more doublings, right?) and secondly, stocks and stock based funds have historically dramatically outperformed bonds and cash over long periods of time.

- Fees are important and play a role in the long term accumulation of your money. Make sure you understand the fees you are paying in your investments. There is no such thing as a free lunch, but make sure you are getting value for what you are paying.

- Creating a diversified portfolio will help to reduce overall risk and help to smooth out the ups and downs of the market

- Dollar cost averaging is a strategy to buy fewer shares when they are more expensive and more shares when they are cheaper. By virtue of the payroll deduction feature of 403(b), 401(k) and 457(b) plans, you are automatically dollar cost averaging, whether you realize it or not!

CHAPTER 4

ACCUMULATION IN NON-RETIREMENT ACCOUNTS / INTERMEDIATE TERM INVESTING

THE FINANCIAL PLANNING PYRAMID (INTERMEDIATE TERM INVESTMENTS)

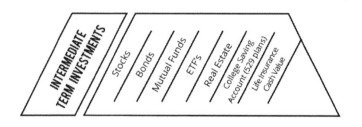

Ok, now that we have saving for retirement under control, we can move along to the next area of our planning; accumulation in non-retirement accounts. If you are not able to save enough for retirement, you really shouldn't be applying much money or any money at all to this section. Most educators will not be able to apply a lot of money to this area as most of their free cash flow should be directed into their retirement accounts, which provide nice tax incentives. However, for those that are on track for retirement and possibly maxing out those accounts, this is the area where the remaining cash flow should be directed.

As a reminder, non-retirement accounts are taxable brokerage accounts and managed investment accounts typically holding mutual funds, exchange traded funds, stocks, bonds, etc. We can also see some real estate investment in this area and use of life insurance cash value, particularly for those with higher household incomes.

Taxable Brokerage Accounts and Managed Investment Accounts. As we discussed before, the main benefit of these accounts over retirement accounts is the flexibility to withdraw your money whenever you need it and for whatever reason. However, that flexibility comes at the cost of significant tax breaks associated with the retirement plans. Taxable accounts can hold just about any investment you care to own—stocks, bonds, mutual funds, exchange traded funds, precious metals and other commodities, real estate investment trusts (REITs), master limited partnerships (MLPs), among others.

It is important to grasp that since these investments do not have tax deferred or tax free growth, they will probably be taxed every year. You can be taxed on capital gains, dividends, and taxed as ordinary income (like salary). The tax owed will vary depending on what type of investment it is, your income, and also how long you held an investment before selling it. The point of this chapter is not to get into the details about capital gains tax and dividend taxes (I can sense your eyes glazing over right now), but instead to make you aware that these types of investments are generally not as tax friendly as the retirement plans.

If you are investing in these accounts you should do so after you max out your retirement plans, or if you have a specific reason for needing to access the money before retirement age. Some good examples would be if you are planning to retire early and you are saving a very high percentage of your income to do so. In this case, you would need a lot of money available to your before you hit "retirement age" to pay your bills during the period from which you actually retire, say age 50, to the age you can withdraw from your retirement accounts at age 59.5. Another good example would be that you are investing for a large purchase that you mean to make before retirement such as a boat, vacation home, or child's wedding. Yet another example would be inheritance money or a windfall that comes your way. This money will need to be invested and you may not be able to get it all into tax sheltered retirement plans due to contribution limits.

It is just as important, if not more so in taxable accounts than retirement accounts, to consider how your investments are allocated. Over long periods of time, history indicates that stocks tend to outperform bonds and cash. In shorter time periods this may not be the case. Understand that this is generally speaking and there are exceptions, but stocks tend to be more volatile than bonds and certainly more so than cash. What I mean by volatility is that the prices of these investments tend to fluctuate more. So if you have a very long investment time horizon, 20, 30, 40 years, you can and should allocate some dollars to stocks. If you have a short time horizon like five years or less, you may want to think twice about that. If you need to use the money in less than five years, there is a chance that your stock based investments may be down and you will lose money. You might want to consider bonds, or a combination of stocks and bonds, to help reduce the risk of volatility. If your time horizon is less than two-to-three years, really ask yourself if the juice is worth the squeeze. I think you might just decide (ahem, ahem) that a CD or bank account might be the best place for that short-term money.

Probably the biggest part of this "intermediate term" area of a financial plan for parents is saving for college for their children. A common conversation I have with clients is trying to get them to put their retirement savings before saving for college. It is a natural response to want to put your children first. I get it: I'm a parent. At the time of publishing, my two sons are five and three. We get in the habit of putting them first in everything we do. They eat their meals before us, they get to watch what they want to on TV, our weekend plans are based around them—we want to sacrifice everything for them. Ever go out on a Friday night and have a little too much fun only to wake up several times throughout the night for bathroom trips (the kids, I mean) and then rise and shine at 6am when the kids get up? Fun stuff. So yeah, I get the impulse and the desire to put the kids first.

But here, you can't do it. There's a saying, "there is financial aid for college but there is no financial aid for retirement." I think that pretty much sums it up. As previously mentioned, if you do not have enough saved for retirement, you have two options 1) work longer or 2) die earlier. Both stink, particularly when option one might not really be an option at all. Your employer might be downsizing or you or a family member might have a major health issue that requires that you quit or retire.

So if you were to put your children first here and make sure that college was funded at the expense of your retirement fund and you were forced into working much longer than normal, or you were unemployed or underemployed not by your choice, how would your kids feel about that? Talk about a tremendous amount of guilt. They would know, especially when they grow to adults that you are in the situation you are in because you funded their college educations. To add insult to injury, they might not even find suitable employment. To avoid going on and on, let's just agree that you need to give the priority to your own retirement savings before you start saving for the education of your kids.

Now, if you are already on track with your retirement savings and there is extra cash flow each month college savings plans are a great idea. You have some options available to you.

First, and probably most popular, is the 529 college savings plan. This account works similarly to a Roth IRA, only with much higher contribution limits and no income restrictions. You contribute money that has already been taxed and invest in mutual funds. You can pick aggressive funds, or conservative funds. The money accumulates tax free just like a Roth IRA and is distributed tax free when used for qualified higher education expenses such as tuition, room and board, books, etc.

You can contribute automatically out of your checking account each month like an automatic bill pay, in some cases your employer will allow payroll deduction, and you can always write checks to the account whenever you wish. Some people set up an automatic monthly investment with an amount that they know works with their budget and then write checks periodically to deposit money the child received for holidays, birthdays, etc. 529 plans can be set up by the parents, grandparents, aunts, uncles, basically anybody for benefit of the beneficiary, which in this case is the child. However, it is important to know that the funds can be used for adults too, but in the majority of the cases it's money for your kid's college education.

While the tax treatment of 529 plans is extremely attractive, if the funds are not used for higher education expenses, the gain in the account (interest) can be subject to capital gains tax and a penalty. The amount that you invested (your basis) will come back to you tax free. While this may be a turn off to some people, all that is happening here is the preferential tax treatment of the 529 plan is being removed from your investment so that the results more accurately reflect what your money would have grown to had it been invested in a regular taxable brokerage account from the beginning.

Another way around this issue is simply to change the beneficiary on the account. You are allowed to change beneficiaries, so if one of your children ends up not going to college, you can change the beneficiary to another child or even yourself if you want to go back to school.

Each state sponsors their own 529 plan and various investment companies are the custodians of the plans. For example, Maryland might use mutual fund company X, while Louisiana uses Y, and Oregon uses Z. You do not need to use your states' plan; you can use any states plan, but you should know that some states offer tax incentives to use their plan. It is important to be informed about the fee structure of the plan your state has, and what if any tax incentives they offer. Also, it is very important to know that the beneficiary of the plan can use the proceeds to go to school at any accredited higher education institution in the country, so there are no restrictions due to state, public or private, etc.

Many states also offer 529 programs where you can basically buy credits at today's prices to use at some time in the future. This can be an attractive option if you do not want to deal with stock market volatility, want your child to go to school in state, and want your account to be tied to the increase in cost of education. The cost of higher education (tuition, room and board) has been increasing by about 5-6% annually (lower when adjusted for inflation) over the last decade, depending on whether you are looking at private or public schools (http://trends.collegeboard.org).

So the inevitable question is "which one is better?" There is no right answer to this. If you want the most flexibility, and your child is still young and you have a long investing time horizon you might find the investment based account more attractive as the child can use the funds for any school and your account could potentially accumulate at a higher rate.

However, the tuition purchase option takes away the issue of stock market volatility, and if you are getting started saving a bit later, say when your child is 10 or older, then you might find this to be a more attractive option.

There are some other options to save for college, but they are not nearly as popular as the 529 plan.

The Coverdell Education Savings Account allows for modest contributions of $2000 per year, and there are income restrictions as well so you would have to make sure that your income falls beneath the cutoff amount. The benefit of Coverdell ESAs is that the money can also be used for private elementary, middle and high school whereas a 529 is solely for higher education expenses.

Uniform Gifts to Minors (UGMA) and Uniform Transfer to Minors (UTMA) accounts: These accounts do not offer any significant tax breaks, and while they can be used for college funding there are much better options with better tax breaks. Control of these accounts will turn over to the child when they reach the age of majority between ages 18 to 25. In my experience, these accounts are used when you want to save or invest money for your child that is not earmarked for college. For example, some people feel that birthday and holiday gift money should not be used for college; that the child should be able to use it for anything they want like a car or other items that interest them when they are older. This would be a good use of an UTMA/UGMA.

With the incredible cost of education these days it is important that parents do the best they can to save for college after they have their retirement savings on track. This will most likely take the form of a 529 plan; however, it is important to realize from the beginning that you may not be able to fully fund college for your children, especially if you have a large family. This is just the reality of the situation. There are many sources of financial aid available such as grants, loans, work study, scholarships, and ROTC. There is also a growing segment of Americans who feel that college may not be all it's cracked up to be when you consider the amount of debt you take on. Whatever your philosophy may be, it's important to create a plan to accomplish whichever goal you desire. A lot of people share the feeling that they will fund half of college and the child will have to fund the other half through work, scholarships, or loans. There is a good argument to be made that this teaches a valuable lesson in responsibility. Some other people pay a percentage of the cost based on the grades the child makes. The better the grades, the more you fund and vice versa. So,

I encourage you to determine how much of the cost of college you would like to fund, and start planning for it. As soon as your child is old enough, you should probably start the financial reality talk concerning college education so they know what to expect.

Chapter 4 Points to Remember

- You should be on track and saving the appropriate amount for retirement before you start allocating dollars to the Intermediate Term part of the pyramid.
- Taxable accounts like brokerage accounts and managed accounts are attractive in that you can access your money whenever you want without an age requirement, but there are no tax incentives.
- For most parents, once they are saving enough for retirement, most of the remaining funds will be allocated to college savings. 529 plans are sponsored by the states and are different for each state.
- Considering the cost of higher education, it is a real possibility that you won't be able to save enough to fully fund a college education for your children. You are not alone!

CHAPTER 5

The Tip of the Pyramid –

Planning for the Fun Stuff

THE FINANCIAL PLANNING PYRAMID (FUN)

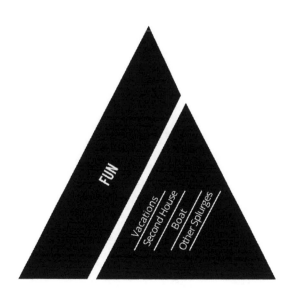

Ok, this will be the shortest chapter in the book, so if you promised yourself that you would at least read one chapter today, you are in luck! You'll be done in just a second and you can reward yourself with a cold one for a job well done.

This is the tip of the financial planning pyramid. The fun stuff, saving for things that don't really have a place in your financial plan but should have a place in your life plan. Do you want to save for an awesome vacation, or do you have a dream of owning a vacation home or a boat? This is where those dreams are addressed. We need to be responsible and address the major concerns in our plan, but if and when they are all adequately addressed, and there is still money left over, we can save for the fun stuff. What you may find is that it is motivating to get to the point that all of your other obligations are being funded and you can save for the fun stuff without any guilt. What you also may find out is that you cannot fund all of your other obligations and also fund the fun stuff. So what do you do now? You might find out that you need to adjust your expectations for retirement and live on less. Maybe you decide to work longer, or work part-time in retirement. Maybe you decide to fund less of your children's college education. Something has to give and everybody makes these difficult decisions differently. What is most important to you? It's your plan.

CHAPTER 6

Estate Planning And Legal Issues

Frequently I include Estate Planning and Legal Issues as part of the bottom or foundation of the pyramid as it can be considered part of the "protection" part of your financial plan. However, in this book I decided to make a separate chapter addressing it. Please note that neither I, nor my firm, offer tax or legal advice. This is for informational purposes only. Please be sure to consult your professional tax and legal advisors regarding your particular circumstances.

As you are accumulating assets and living your life pre-retirement, there are a number of issues that you should be aware of from a legal and estate planning perspective. First, make sure you have a will. It is shocking how many people do not have wills or simply think that their spouse will get everything when they pass. If you do not have a will, the state may determine where your assets go after you are gone. In some states your spouse will not get everything. If you have children, your assets may be split between your spouse and children. If you don't have children, your assets could be split between your spouse and your parents. It just makes for a messy situation. I, for one, do not want the state determining who gets my money after I die. If you feel like I do, get a will. You will also name guardians for your children as part of your will.

While we are talking about wills, please make sure that you have your beneficiary designations updated and coordinated with your will. In contracts or accounts with named beneficiaries like retirement accounts (pensions, IRAs, 403(b)'s, etc.) and life insurance, the benefits will pass to whomever is named as the beneficiary regardless of what your will indicates. Remember your ex-husband who you can't even stand to speak to? If you named him as your beneficiary years ago and never updated your beneficiary designations, he will receive those assets when you die. Oops!

Next, you should strongly consider a living will. This is a legal document that indicates which life saving measures, if any, should be pursued in the event of a catastrophic illness or injury. When to pull the plug? Everybody has different feelings about this matter and none are wrong or right. I'd like to take a second just to point out that a living WILL (what we are talking about now) is different from a living TRUST. This tends to be a point of confusion for many people. We will discuss living trusts later in the book. A living will is incredibly important for many reasons. I know that some of you are thinking "my spouse and I have had this talk many times and he or she knows exactly what I want to have done." Well, sometimes it's not always that clear. Sometimes the condition and the chances of recovery are not exactly how you may have planned. It will be a very stressful situation for your family if you are ever in a situation in which someone will need to make a decision as to whether you will live or die. It will make the decision makers' life much less stressful if they are simply following the directions that you put forward and signed in your living will.

Let's go through two different scenarios that you may or may not have thought about. In the first scenario, you are in a situation where it does not appear that you will recover, but there is a slight chance that you will. You and your spouse have discussed this situation before and your spouse knows that you would want to discontinue life-continuation measures. So your spouse tells the doctors to discontinue life support, but your parents disagree with this decision.

They are furious and crying their eyes out, screaming at your spouse and calling them a murderer. In this scenario, all your spouse is doing is trying to carry out your wishes. However, your parents weren't aware of your wishes. Having a living will would have solved this problem because your spouse could have simply shown the document to your parents and said "I don't want to do this anymore than you do, but I am simply carrying out his/her wishes".

Another scenario would assume that this situation occurred later in life when perhaps you have children that are school age. You can understand the confusion, hurt and anger that the kids might feel to your spouse, possibly for the rest of their lives, when your spouse decides to carry out your wishes to discontinue life preservation measures. In your children's eyes it could be seen as mommy is killing daddy, or vice versa. It would be immensely helpful to be able to explain to the kids that this is in fact what mommy wanted, and here it is where she signed that this is what she wanted.

Look, this is a situation that nobody ever wishes on anybody and hopefully you will never have to go through it. Unfortunately, it does happen, and if the proper preparation and documentation is not in place it has the potential to destroy families and relationships. This can easily be avoided by having a living will.

Another document you should have is a durable power of attorney for financial matters. This document assigns somebody power of attorney over you in the event you become incapacitated and unable to make financial decisions on your own behalf.

A durable power of attorney for healthcare is also important. This document assigns somebody power of attorney over you to work with doctors and other healthcare providers to ensure you get the care you need if and when you become incapacitated.

Lastly, I would recommend that you set up a trust as part of your will. This is also known as a testamentary trust. This can help address many potential problems.

Problem #1: You pass away and leave behind children who are minors.

In my experience, most people who have minor children set up the beneficiary information on their retirement plans and life insurance like this:

> Primary Beneficiary: My Spouse
> Contingent Beneficiary: My kids

Well, if your kids are three and five years old, they will not get the money outright; it will go into the care of their guardians until they reach the age of majority. This can be problematic, and at the very least, tempting for the guardians to abuse. Remember, if you have minor children and you are following the first step of setting up a financial plan correctly, you and your spouse should have considerable life insurance. You should also have retirement plan balances and investment accounts. If you both die together in an accident, this would provide quite a bit of money, a couple to several million dollars in some cases.

If you have a trust set up the beneficiary information will be set up like this:

> Primary Beneficiary: My Spouse
> Contingent Beneficiary: My Trust under my last will and testament

So now what happens is this: If you OR your spouse dies, the assets transfer to the surviving spouse. If you both die together, the trust receives all of the assets. The assets will be managed by the trustees you select, according to how you indicated in the trust documents. The assets will also be distributed by the trustees according to how you indicated in the trust documents.

Here is a sample scenario of how one could structure their trust terms. The guardians of the children will automatically be distributed X amount of dollars each month for the care of the children. Any expense for education or medical expenses is automatically approved. At the age of 25, a third of the trust assets will be available to the beneficiaries of the trust (the kids), at the age of 30 the next third will be available, and at age 35 the remainder of the assets will be available to the beneficiaries. This provision can help alleviate the potential problem of the kids getting all the trust money at age 18 and blowing it all in a short period of time because they are young and immature. Any distribution above and beyond these terms must be approved by the trustee. The trustee can either be a corporate trustee at a bank and trust company (for a fee), or they can be another family member like a grandparent, aunt or uncle of the children. By setting it up this way, you create a system of checks and balances so that the guardians cannot access or abuse the assets for your children.

Problem #2: You pass away and leave behind children who are adults.

Huh? What's the problem here? My kids are adults when I pass, so what's the big deal?

What if one or more of your adult children isn't the best with money? It slips through their fingers like sand, and you know that they will squander or waste their whole inheritance in a short period of time. If the trust receives the money and not your children outright, you can control how the money can be distributed from the trust even after you pass away. Cool, huh?

What if you love your child but can't stand their spouse? If you leave your money to your child outright, their spouse also just hit the lottery. You didn't really want that to happen, right? If the trust receives it, you can protect the assets from your child's spouse (who you say you love, but really can't stand! —shh, I won't tell, I promise!)

What if your child has debts or is in trouble with creditors? A trust can help protect the assets from the creditors as well.

Wills, living wills, powers of attorney, and trusts: I highly recommend all of these documents as part of your estate planning while you are younger and raising a family AND when you are older and protecting your family. They can help prevent many serious issues that can come up when a tragedy occurs. For those who are confident in their abilities or are do-it-yourselfers there are online services available to help guide you in the creation of these documents. For those with more complicated situations or those who prefer to work with a professional, find a qualified estate planning attorney to help you with the process.

The last topic I would like to touch on in this chapter is death taxes. Death taxes usually refer to three different taxes. I will give a brief overview of them here but these taxes change frequently, so use this mainly as a guideline and make sure you consult with a qualified tax advisor for your specific situation.

1) **Federal Estate Tax**. Tax levied by the Federal government on your right to transfer assets to your heirs after your death. This tax currently only comes into play if your estate is worth more than about $5,430,000 if you are single, or $10,860,000, if married as of 2015. If you are fortunate enough to have an estate in excess of these limits, a tax will be levied on the excess. The top tax rate in 2015 is 40% (ouch!)

2) **State Estate Tax**. Tax levied by a state government on your right to transfer assets to your heirs after your death. Note: Not all states have state estate taxes and the states that do have wildly varying exemption amounts and tax rates. Consult with a qualified tax advisor.

3) **State Inheritance Tax**. Similar to but different from State Estate Tax, this tax is based on who receives the assets and their relation to the deceased. Note: Not all states have state inheritance tax and those that do have varying exemption amounts and tax rates. Consult with a qualified tax advisor.

Chapter 6 Points To Remember

- Everyone should have basic estate planning documents set up. These are a will, living will, Durable Power of Attorney, and a trust as part of your will (testamentary trust).
- A last Will and Testament indicates to the court to whom you would like your property to pass.
- Make sure that your beneficiary designations are up to date and coordinate with your will.
- A living will indicates your wishes regarding life continuation measures.
- Power of attorney gives somebody the authorization to make decisions (financial and/or health related) on your behalf if you are incapacitated and cannot make decisions on your own.
- A testamentary trust is important if so that your assets go where you want them to go and are protected from certain abuses and unintended uses.
- Death Taxes are the commonly used "catch all" term for Federal Estate Tax, and State Estate and Inheritance taxes. All of these taxes change frequently, so it is best to consult with a qualified tax advisor to determine what affects you and in what capacity.

SECTION I

CONCLUSION

This concludes the first part of the book. So far we covered how to help protect your assets with correct insurance products and coverage. We discussed how to accumulate retirement assets through employer sponsored plans and IRA's. We reviewed various other investments and the pros and cons of each. We discussed saving for your children's education and some basic estate planning documents that everybody should have. In the second part of the book, we will examine the issues you need to be aware of at the point of retirement and throughout your life in retirement including distribution planning, tax implications, Social Security and Medicare, and estate planning concerning transitioning assets to the next generation. If you are a younger reader and do not have the desire to learn about these issues at this point, you can stop reading. However, I highly recommend that you continue and finish the book. The second section is full of important information and will help solidify everything that we just learned.

SECTION II

To Retirement... and Beyond!

I n this section we will cover the issues you will face as you transition into retirement. We will cover expenses and income sources, creating cash flows from your retirement accounts, and other investments and social programs such as Social Security and Medicare. We will discuss long-term care issues and estate planning as it applies to transferring wealth upon your death and legacy planning. Even if you are a younger reader and these issues seem light years away, I highly recommend that you read this section. It will only take a couple hours of your time, and it will reinforce everything that you've learned so far and put it into context.

CHAPTER 7

EXPENSES IN RETIREMENT

What you will notice in retirement is that some expenses decrease or are eliminated entirely, while some expenses increase or appear for the first time. There are some expenses that you will incur regardless of what stage you are in life. You will always need to eat. You will always need to pay for transportation whether you own a vehicle or choose public transportation. Utilities of some sort will probably always be present, and as they say, the only two things that are certain in life are death and taxes, so you will always be faced with taxes.

However, you will notice that some expenses will (should) fall away. Your children will be grown and independent. You shouldn't be paying student loans for yourself anymore, the mortgage could very well be paid off, you get the idea. Some expenses may still exist, but should be smaller by retirement age. You might see savings in the way of gasoline because you are no longer driving to work every day. Your clothing budget might shrink, too. If you downsize your house, you might enjoy lower utility costs and property taxes.

You will also notice that some expenses increase. Healthcare and prescription drug costs could and probably will increase. You may spend more money on travel and leisure activities than in the past. Some expenses will emerge for the first time. You may find yourself financially supporting your elderly parents. You will need to address your own financial responsibility for long-term care or skilled care whether it is through long-term care insurance or other means. These expenses may be new to you but need to be addressed in your budgeting.

Your income sources may include Social Security, pension income, retirement plans like 403(b), 457(b), 401(k), and IRAs both traditional and Roth. You may also have other investments in taxable accounts and cash value in life insurance policies. Maybe you have been involved in real estate investing over the years and have positive cash flow from rental properties. Inheritances and part-time work could round out the income sources.

The main challenge in retirement is cash flow. You need to make sure that you have enough coming in each month in a sustainable way to cover your expenses. In order to do this properly, you need to have a really good idea of what your projected expenses will be in retirement and you need to have a margin of error in those calculations to account for the unknown and for discretionary purchases. Then you need to make sure that this cash flow can increase at a satisfactory pace to maintain your purchasing power in retirement due to inflation of your expenses and any possible changes in tax policy in the future. You don't want your income to be so close to your expenses that if taxes were to increase you would suddenly find yourself in trouble.

Many retirees find it helpful to pay off as much debt as possible before retirement (mortgage) and also to replace many aging appliances and other large ticket items (cars, new windows, roof, etc.). This can be an effective strategy for a couple of reasons. First, it makes budgeting and cash flow forecasting much easier because you have less monthly expenses. Second, it creates peace of mind and gives a psychological boost to help you transition into retirement. It's hard to lose the house if you own it free and clear, right? You might also reason that if you have a fully paid off car with 30,000 miles on it and you only put on 8,000 miles per year that it will last you a long time before it needs to be replaced. If you replace an aging roof with 50-year shingles, you shouldn't have to replace it ever again. Eliminating the big ticket purchases can clearly help you feel more confident as you transition into retirement.

Some other retirees will choose to go about it a different way. If someone possesses sufficient financial knowledge and has the assets and cash flow to make us both comfortable with the strategy, sometimes I will recommend that they essentially do the exact opposite with liabilities (mortgage and car loans). Why? Because we are currently in a very low interest rate environment, which means that borrowing money is cheap.

But, we usually need to do a little deprogramming first. You see, nearly everyone in the baby boomer generation has been programmed to think that paying off the mortgage as early as possible is a smart financial move. I will not argue with the psychological aspect of that. There is incredible confidence and peace of mind that comes with not having any debt. However, if we look at the purely financial side of it, it may not be in your best interest to aggressively pay off that mortgage or auto loan. Let's use the mortgage, for example. At the time I am writing this book, someone with good credit can get a mortgage for around 4% for a 30-year fixed rate. So let's use 4% as our example. We know that over long periods of time, inflation has been around 3%. So really, our interest rate is just about 1% above inflation. That is cheap. Darn cheap. Let's let that sink in and really understand it.

A bank is willing to let you borrow money, and a lot of it, for 30 years at around 1% above the inflation rate. Hmmm. What else do we know? Historically speaking, over long periods of time, the stock market has returned just around 10%. So does it stand to reason that if I were to pay just the minimum payment on the mortgage and allocate the "extra money" that I would normally apply to the mortgage to pay it off early to another investment such as an index fund that I may be better off in the long run? Possibly.

So why is everyone programmed to pay off their mortgage early? Well, most of these folks spent the bulk of their working and adult years in the late 70s, 80s, 90s and early 2000s. Interest rates were a lot higher then. A mortgage in the early 80s might have been 15%. Even throughout the 80s, 90s and early 2000s, interest rates were a lot higher than today. So, let's say the mortgage had an interest rate of 8%. It would probably still be good advice to pay off the mortgage early, or certainly before retirement. You could avoid paying an 8% interest rate by allocating extra dollars to paying off the mortgage, or you could possibly get a non-guaranteed rate of return of something similar if you allocate the extra money to stock market investments; but you also get all the volatility and stomach churning that the market provides. In this case, I feel a bird in the hand is worth two in the bush. Stop paying the 8% and pay off the mortgage early. As an added bonus, you get the psychological boost of being out of debt. This is why it has been standard teaching to pay off mortgages early.

However, currently we are in a historically low interest rate environment. Those with financial acumen and the risk tolerance might be able to accumulate some significant additional wealth by leveraging those extra dollars into other investments.

There are some significant caveats here.

1) I feel that the interest rates on the debt have to be very low for this strategy to work well over time. As interest rates rise in the future this may not be the best strategy.

2) You must be disciplined in investing the extra money each month. You cannot spend it elsewhere. If you do not have this discipline, then allocate the extra dollars to your mortgage each month. Paying off your mortgage is a form of discipline similar to that in a 403(b) or 401(k) plan where the money is automatically saved each month, saving yourself from yourself.

3) Markets are volatile, and you need to have the patience and self-discipline not to withdraw your investment money if and when the market goes down.

4) You must be very good at budgeting and managing your cash flow in retirement.

5) You need to be comfortable transitioning into retirement with debt.

Some of the most significant expenses in retirement will be those associated with healthcare and long- term care.

Healthcare

If you retire before age 65 you will need to arrange for health insurance until age 65 when you are covered by Medicare (www.medicare.gov). You may be able to stay on your employer's group plan until age 65 whether it is your school district, college or university, or private school. This in many cases will be your best bet. Because it is a group plan the coverage levels tend to be better than other plans and the premium, while still expensive is typically less than other options. In some cases, your contract may include healthcare coverage to age 65. If you have this in your contract, consider yourself lucky and pay particularly close attention to contract negotiations in the future because you might lose this benefit.

Other options to explore would be the healthcare exchanges a la Obamacare. Depending on your income, these could potentially provide good coverage at an attractive premium.

If your spouse is still working, you could and should look into jumping on their health plan through their employer.

Whichever option you choose, you should make sure that you have coverage, uninterrupted until age 65. Make sure that you understand what your health plan covers and what you are responsible for regarding co-pays, coinsurance, deductibles, etc. Remember, there is no such thing as a "free lunch," and a cheaper monthly premium typically means higher out of pocket expenses. In retirement the doctor visits typically increase, medication and prescriptions tend to increase, and medical procedures tend to increase (National Institute on Aging). It is always a trade-off between paying a higher monthly premium for more comprehensive coverage or paying a lesser monthly premium for less comprehensive coverage and the potential for higher out of pocket expenses. Pick your poison.

While nobody has a crystal ball, typically if you are in good health and don't take medications, you might be better off picking a plan with a lower premium and higher out of pocket expenses under the thought process that you don't go to the doctors much anyway. The reverse would hold true as well. If you have several medications, and see the doctor frequently, it would probably be in your best interest just to pay a higher premium and less out of pocket.

At age 65 you apply for Medicare. You've been paying for it all along through your payroll taxes, so now you can cash in! The downside is that now you are old enough for Medicare. Medicare gets to be pretty complicated and detailed. The mission of this book is to give you the main issues you need to grasp while keeping the subject matter light and fast moving. I will give a brief overview of Medicare, but understand that it is far from exhaustive (on purpose).

Medicare provides health care benefits but does still include premiums, copays, and coinsurance. It is important to understand that Medicare was never designed to cover all healthcare expenses. In fact, there is no limit to out of pocket costs that are not covered under Medicare. Because of this, it is important to consider a Medicare supplement insurance plan, also called a Medigap plan. These plans coordinate with the Medicare benefits to limit the out of pocket expenses that you may incur.

Medicare Part A enrollment is automatic and mandatory if you are already receiving Social Security. If not, you can initially enroll in the three months prior to your 65th birthday month, the month of your birthday, and the three months following. This is a seven-month period.

You can also enroll during a special enrollment period, which are the eight months after the first month that either your employment ends or your group health coverage ends.

Last, the general enrollment period each year is from January 1 to March 31. Coverage begins July 1.

Medicare Part B is VOLUNTARY. Most people will enroll in both A and B at the same time. However, if you are already receiving Social Security, you will automatically be enrolled in part B just like part A. If you do not want to be enrolled in part B you will have to opt out. The initial enrollment period is the same seven-month window previously described for part A. The special enrollment period is the same as well, and the annual enrollment period is also the same.

Medicare A and B cover different health services and expenses. This is beyond the scope of this book and a simple internet search will give you the differences.

Medicare Part D covers prescription drug costs. Medicare parts A and B have very limited coverage for drug costs so most people should enroll in D as well to cover possibly catastrophic out of pocket drug costs in retirement. You can initially enroll in D when you become eligible for Medicare. After that, the annual enrollment period is October 15 through December 7.

Each part D plan offers different levels of coverage and also has different formularies (what drugs it covers). It is incredibly important to make sure that any drugs you are currently taking and any drugs you may be taking in the next year are covered under the plans formulary.

When you consider the premium expense, cost sharing, tiers of drugs in the formulary and many other factors it becomes obvious that you need to do your homework to find the plan that is best suited to you and your drug needs for the best price.

Medigap plans, also known as Medicare supplement plans provide coverage for the "gaps" in coverage with Medicare. There are A, B, C, D, F, G, K, L, M and N. These coverages are uniform. For example, Medigap policy A offered by one insurance company covers the same as Medigap policy A from another insurance company. There are some "core benefits" that all Medigap policies are required to cover, but after that there are differences between the policies. It is important to educate yourself on the differences and make sure you choose the policy that most closely aligns with your needs.

Healthcare expenses will make up a large portion of most retirees total expenses in retirement. It has been estimated that on average a 65-year-old couple can expect to pay over $200,000 in out of pocket healthcare expenses in retirement. It is important to plan for this and budget properly.

Long-Term Care

One of the biggest concerns of retirees and those transitioning into retirement is the issue of long-term care. Long-term care is not typically medical care but instead assistance with the basic personal tasks of life such as bathing, dressing, personal hygiene, using the toilet, maintaining continence, eating, walking, maintaining mobility, and getting in and out of a bed or chair. *Long-term care is not typically covered by Medicare.* Usually you need to pay out of pocket for expenses until your assets are depleted to the point that you are under the poverty line. At this point you would qualify for coverage under Medicaid (note: Medicaid; not Medicare) (http://longtermcare.gov).

While most people think of nursing homes when they think of long-term care, it is important to understand that a lot of this type of care can also be done at adult day care centers, assisted living facilities and at home. Everybody needs a plan for long-term care. Most people can be categorized into one of three groups.

1) Those who have very little assets and should simply let Medicaid and the state take their assets if they need long-term care.

2) Those who have assets to protect in the event of a long-term care stay. These people need to strongly consider long-term care insurance in some capacity.

3) Those who have considerable assets and can afford to self-insure or pay out of pocket if and when the need arises.

Let's talk about the first group. These are the folks who do not have a lot of assets. Maybe they own their home and have some modest savings and investments. For these people, they probably shouldn't bother getting long-term care insurance because the premiums would be too high for their budget and they don't have sufficient assets to protect, anyway. Now, that being said, some of these folks may still choose to purchase coverage for other reasons. They may want to make sure that they get a certain level of care, or that they can pay for home healthcare, or they may simply want to protect whatever assets they have for their children out of principle. It is important to note that long-term care premiums are often less expensive if you apply when you are younger. So for people who are concerned about large premiums fitting into their monthly budget, they may want to consider applying for coverage at a younger age.

The second group have more assets to protect. Let's give an example of $500,000 to $1,000,000 in savings and investments—they want to make sure that they don't lose all of their money in the event of a long-term care issue. With the cost of care being upwards of $100,000 per year and rising, and the average duration of need being about three years (www.longtermcare.gov), one can see how this type of expense can quickly deplete a portfolio, particularly if both spouses end up needing care. This can deplete the amount of money they can pass to their heirs and possibly even threaten the standard of living of a spouse who is not receiving care. For example, consider a married couple; the wife needs care for four years at about $400,000. If they started with $500,000 in assets, now there is only $100k left for the husband to live on for the rest of his life. This is a bad situation in and of itself; but if he eventually needs care, the remaining assets will disappear.

The third group are high net worth families. Let's use an example of $5,000,000 and higher in assets. They can afford to self-insure if they choose. What I mean by self-insure is they can simply pay out of pocket if care is needed. Even if the cost is $1,000,000 for both spouses to have care they still have $4,000,000 left to pass to their heirs. However, it is interesting to note that many of these people still choose to insure against the risk of long-term care. Nobody likes the idea of losing serious wealth due to a long-term care event.

At this point I bet everyone is really pumped to keep talking about long-term care because it is such an uplifting subject, right? Ok, so now you need to know that roughly 70% of all people will need care at some point in their life (www.nihseniorhealth.gov). Women have a higher chance of needing care than men and their average duration of care is slightly longer than men, too. Why? Because women live longer (www.nihseniorhealth.gov).

While advances in modern medicine are undoubtedly wonderful, they have created more of a long-term care issue. With people living longer, the need for care is greater. Roughly 40% of long-term care claims are now cognitively related, read Alzheimer's and dementia (www.genworth.com). So, with a 70% care rate, particularly if you are married, you need to plan for your, and/or your spouse's eventual care.

You may be saying to yourself that you will provide the care for your spouse and your spouse will provide the care for you if you need it. What I'd like you to think about is how you are planning to get your spouse out of the bathtub when you are ninety years old. How will your spouse help you off the toilet? What will your life be like if you can never leave your spouse who has developed Alzheimer's because you are afraid that they will wander off and not be able to find their way home, or fear that they will burn the house down try-ing to microwave a frying pan? Will the kids take care of you? Better question: Do you really want to put them through that? They may live in another state. They surely will be busy with their own careers and family. Do you want them to spend their retirement years caring for you and not being able to enjoy their lives? Nobody wants to think about this stuff, but it's very serious.

There are a couple different ways to insure against the cost of long-term care. They are either "stand alone" long-term care insurance or hybrid products. Both kinds of insurance usually start paying benefits after you can no longer do two or more activities of daily living (ADL's) (www.money.usnews.com). The ADL's are:

- Bathing
- Dressing
- Personal Hygiene
- Using the toilet
- Maintaining continence
- Eating
- Walking
- Maintaining mobility inside the home
- Transferring into or out of a bed, chair, or wheelchair.

Most policies also usually trigger benefits for cognitive issues such as Alzheimer's and dementia independent of the other ADL's.

Stand Alone Long-Term Care Insurance
Stand-alone long-term care insurance is what most people have heard about and possibly have even looked into. The way it works is you pay a premium (monthly, quarterly, semi-annually, or annually) in exchange you will receive a per diem or monthly dollar amount to pay for your care if and when you need it. There are a couple different variables that determine how much your premium will be.

The main variables are:

- Benefit Amount: How much benefit do you want per day or per month?

- Benefit Duration: How many years do you want this benefit to last? Typical choices are 1, 3, and 5 years.
- Elimination Period: How long do you want to wait until benefits begin? Typical choices are 90, 180, or 365 days with 90 days being very popular. Note: The longer your elimination period, the lower your premium will be but you will need to pay out of pocket, or provide the bulk of care yourself during this time.
- Cost of Living Adjustment (COLA): This increases the amount of your benefit at a certain percentage each year to attempt to keep pace with the increasing cost of care. It is almost always a good idea to get a COLA, particularly if you purchase your policy when you are younger because there would in theory be many more years before you would need care and the cost of care can rise significantly during this time. A lot of policies have different COLA choices these days and they will all affect the premium differently. For example, there can be a simple interest or compound interest COLA, and they can be offered with different interest rates too.
- Shared Care Rider: Basically allows spouses to dip into each other's pool of money if they need extra.
- Age at which you obtain coverage: Premiums are generally less expensive the younger you are.

These stand-alone policies typically offer significant discounts if both spouses buy coverage. However, the two main downsides and concerns about these policies are the following:

1) If you don't use it, you lose it. If you don't need care and you just don't wake up one morning, you don't get any benefit out of it. You've paid premiums for many years for nothing. By the way, I don't know of anybody who would rather go through a long-term care stay just to get a benefit out of their policy, and while we can't talk to the dead to ask their opinion, I'm pretty sure they are fine with it. (On a side note: I think it

is important to point out that your auto, homeowners, disability income, and umbrella policies work the same way. You pay premiums every year, but if you don't get into a horrific car accident, or have your house burn down, or become disabled, or have somebody sue you for falling on your front step, you don't get any real benefit from them. If you don't use it, you lose it. But millions upon millions of people have these coverages, so why is this issue such a hang-up about long-term care insurance?)

2) Premiums aren't guaranteed. The insurance companies reserve the right to raise premiums in the future. To be clear, they can't raise just *your* premium, they have to do it to a whole class of policyholders. This has happened in the past and could potentially happen in the future so it is something to be aware of as it can affect your budgeting in retirement.

Hybrid Products

Hybrid products can be an attractive alternative to stand-alone long-term care insurance. They can be annuities with long-term care benefits or permanent life insurance policies with long-term care benefits. The vast majority of these products are life insurance contracts with optional long-term care riders available at an additional cost, so we will briefly discuss how they work.

Basically how these products work is you buy a permanent life insurance policy and pay a bit more for a long-term care rider that allows you to utilize your own death benefit before you die to help pay for long-term care expenses. Let's say you purchase a $500,000 policy with a long-term care rider. If you need long-term care, you would have a $500,000 pool of money available to pay for your care. If you don't use all of the money, the remainder gets paid out to your beneficiary as life insurance death benefit proceeds. Example: you need care and you spend $200,000 of your death benefit on long-term care and then pass away. Your beneficiary would get a check for $300,000 as the remainder of the death benefit. If you don't need care at all, your beneficiary gets all $500,000 as a life insurance death benefit. Death benefits are generally free from income taxes.

It is a solution that many people find very attractive because if the policy is structured correctly, it solves the problems of traditional stand-alone long-term care.

1) "If you don't use it you lose it." Well, now that is not an issue. If you don't use it, your beneficiary gets the death benefit.
2) "Premiums aren't guaranteed and can be raised in the future." With the life insurance policy, as long as it is designed properly, this should not be a problem.

The main downside to this type of arrangement is that it often costs more than stand-alone long-term care insurance. You can fund these policies in varying ways. Some work better with a lump sum drop in. Say you have $100,000 sitting in a low earning CD or savings account; you could make a one-time payment to one of these policies and leverage it into a certain amount of money that can be available to help offset the costs of long-term care. Some other policies are set up to be better with ongoing premium payments like a traditional life insurance policy.

Another strategy is to repurpose existing permanent life insurance coverage. What I mean by this is if you currently have a permanent policy, whether it is whole life or universal life, you can generally do what is called a 1035 exchange (like a rollover) of the cash value of your old policy into a new policy with a long-term care rider. You'd be configuring that older policy into a much more versatile tool going forward. Please note that these transfers may have fees or charges associated with them, but are definitely worth looking into. A qualified advisor can help you navigate the transfer landscape and make a good decision on which policy might be best for you.

Most people end up applying for long-term care coverage in their 50s. It is worth mentioning that underwriting is becoming increasingly difficult as some insurers have exited the marketplace, and those who remain have reduced the amount of risk they are willing to take on. You may want to consider applying at an earlier age to get a better health rating, cheaper premiums, or simply to ensure that you are accepted for coverage.

A big question is how much benefit to purchase. Whether you are pursuing stand-alone coverage or a hybrid product, the cost of your premiums will largely depend on the benefit amount. If you buy enough to cover every contingency, the insurance can get prohibitively expensive. If you buy too little, you will wish you hadn't in the event that you need care. Usually, the answer lies somewhere in between. Often the answer is found by figuring out how much you can afford to pay out of pocket and how comfortable you are using your own assets. Then, buy enough to bridge that gap and hedge the risk. As a basic example let's say it costs around $100,000 per year for care in your area. Going over your assets and budget with your advisor you feel comfortable paying $30,000 per year for care. In this scenario, you should apply for $70,000-$80,000 of benefits per year with a COLA.

Healthcare issues can make up a huge portion of your expenses in retirement, so it is critical that you understand what we have covered in this chapter. As much as we don't want to dwell on something as depressing as long-term care and medical expenses, taking the proper course of action now might save you from a world of financial pain later.

Other significant expenses in retirement besides the usual monthly expenses could be the financial support of other family members such as your aging relatives. Many do not have a financial plan and do not have a lot of money in retirement. You may find yourself in a position where someone close to you needs help. This needs to be considered in your planning. Also, you may find yourself still financially supporting your children if they fall on tough times. Again, these possibilities need to be taken into account.

Ok, so now we have all of these expenses and possible expenses in retirement. How do we pay for them?

Chapter 7 Points to Remember:

- Your expenses will be different than while you were working. Some will be eliminated; some will be reduced. Some will increase, and some will be introduced.
- Healthcare and long-term care will be huge expenses in retirement for most people.
- Typical income sources in retirement are Social Security, pensions, and retirement accounts like 403(b)'s and IRAs. To a lesser degree, brokerage accounts (holding stocks, bonds, mutual funds, etc.), life insurance cash values, and real estate.
- Cash flow makes or breaks a retirement plan.
- Some find it helpful to eliminate as much debt as possible before retirement and to replace aging appliances and complete large and costly home repairs before retirement.
- Medicare will come into play at age 65. A Medicare supplement is very important to limit out of pocket costs.
- Long-term care expenses are generally not covered by Medicare. You need to have a plan for this.

CHAPTER 8

INCOME IN RETIREMENT

I ncome is the lifeblood of your retirement. As mentioned before, if you do not have enough income in retirement, you have two choices 1) work longer or 2) die earlier. Now, depending on whom you are married to, you may actually like those choices, but most of us would rather pick option number 3 which is to have enough income to live the life we want to in retirement.

So now we are at picture taking time. Did you do a good job saving and investing throughout your working years? Can you sit back and enjoy the life you want to live because you sacrificed and made responsible choices when you were younger? There is so much talk today about the magic number needed to retire. Let me save you some time here. There is no magic number. That number is different for every single person and household. The number depends first and foremost on what your monthly expenses look like. How big of a nut do we need to deal with every month? The number also has to do with how old you are when you retire and how long you end up living. While we can do our best to forecast how long you will live, nobody knows for sure. What we do know is that people are living longer, and provided you take care of yourself and avoid some damaging health habits, you should expect to live a long time, too.

Let's go through your typical income sources in retirement.

Social Security. Some teachers are covered by Social Security and some aren't. It is extremely important to find out if you are covered by going to www.socialsecurity.gov and setting up your account online. Also, if you are subject to the Government Pension Offset (GPO) or the Windfall Elimination Provision (WEP) it is important to know how these issues will affect your Social Security benefits. Both GPO and WEP were discussed earlier in the book.

I could write a whole book on Social Security, many have and God bless them. I have zero desire to do this, so let's just put it this way: Social Security can be very complicated and has lots of ins and outs ranging from who is covered, to different claiming strategies, to survivor benefits to divorce situations and on and on. I cannot stress enough the need to work with a competent advisor when it comes to Social Security. The decisions that you make here are very important.

What I intend to do in this section is discuss Social Security in generalities that will apply to most folks. This should not be considered the unabridged definitive guide to Social Security. I am just trying to get you the basics without making your eyes cross in your head and putting you to sleep.

For all its shortcomings, Social Security will end up being a significant part of many people's retirement income. Again, I don't subscribe to the idea that Social Security will be bankrupt. It might change a bit, but I don't think we will see the day when a President says in the State of the Union Address "oh by the way, we were really irresponsible and mismanaged your money and Social Security is bankrupt." What I can say about Social Security is that it provides a steady monthly paycheck backed by the US government, and it contains a cost of living adjustment. This is hugely powerful when we need to produce rising income over potentially a third of a century in retirement.

If you are covered by Social Security, your online statement will show your estimated monthly benefit from age 62 (early retirement) to full retirement age (sliding scale based on your birthdate- generally around age 66-67 for most people reading this) all the way up to age 70.

If you decide to take Social Security benefits before your full retirement age, they will be reduced permanently. You have the ability to take benefits as early as age 62 but this will give you the lowest possible payment for the rest of your life. If you choose to delay Social Security past full retirement age you can continue to accrue deferral credits and your payment will get larger up until age 70.

While it is tempting to take early retirement and thus a lower monthly payment from Social Security some people would be better served to wait until full retirement age, potentially even liquidating some other assets to bridge the income gap from the age you stop working to the point that you are full retirement age for Social Security. This will provide a higher income stream for you, with a cost of living adjustment into your later years of retirement.

If you do not have a large Social Security benefit, or any benefit at all, you can take spousal benefits of 50% off of your spouse's record. For example, if your spouse is entitled to $2000 per month from Social Security, you can receive $1000 per month as well. This could be affected if you are subject to Government Pension Offset (GPO) mentioned previously in the book.

If your spouse dies before you, you can choose to take the higher of the two payments. Example: You have benefits of $1500 monthly and your spouse has $2000 monthly. If he/she dies first, then you can bump up to $2000 monthly. (www.socialsecurity.gov) This could also be affected if you are subject to Government Pension Offset (GPO).

If you decide to take early retirement from Social Security and continue to work either full time or in a part time job, you may be surprised to find out that your Social Security benefit may be reduced. You are allowed to make up to a certain amount of earned income (think salary or hourly wages) in a year before Social Security reduces your benefit. The amount you are allowed to earn can change every year, but to give you an idea of how much you can earn, the limit is $15,720 in 2015. (www.socialsecurity.gov)

So, if you take early retirement from Social Security you can make up to $15,720 of earned income before your Social Security benefits are reduced. They will be reduced by $1 for every $2 you earn over the limit of $15,720 from the time you start collecting benefits until the year that you turn full retirement age (assuming that you are continuing to work and make over the earnings threshold every year). In the year that you turn full retirement age, the earnings limit increases sharply ($41,880 in 2015) and the reduction is reduced to $1 for every $3 over the limit. Starting in the month you turn full retirement age, there are no limitations on how much you can make in earned income. Your Social Security benefit will not be reduced. (www.socialsecurity.gov)

Many people believe that this reduction is a penalty and they will forever lose the benefits that were reduced. This is not the case. At full retirement age Social Security will recalculate and increase your benefit, taking into consideration the prior reduction in benefits. It is also important to know that the income limit applies to EARNED INCOME; not pension income or investment income. It should really only affect you if you have pulled the trigger on Social Security early (before full retirement age) and continue to work either full time, or part-time such that you are making over $15,720 from work.

Pension Plans. Many teachers, particularly public school teachers have a pension. While these can take many forms like 401(a) plans and Cash Balance plans, for this section we are referring to traditional defined benefit pension plans where there is one large pension fund and the benefit that you will receive annually in retirement is derived from a formula. You will receive this payment every month until you die, and depending on what options you choose, you can provide a lifetime income stream to your survivor as well.

First, you need to find out if you are covered by a pension, and if so, what the formula is. Also make sure that you know if your pension has a cost of living adjustment. Most do not, but you should look into it anyway. If you are at the point that you are planning for retirement in a couple years, or this year, I would assume (hope?) that you already know whether you have a pension and if so what the formula is.

For most people the easiest and most accurate way to find out what you can expect from your pension is to request a retirement estimate from the pension fund itself. You might be able to do this online when you are logged into your pension systems' website. They will use information such as your gender, age, years of service and salary information to generate your estimate. To generate data for survivorship options you will be asked for age and gender of your survivor annuitant. This is typically your spouse.

For most plans you will be offered several options. You will likely be offered a Single Life Annuity and various Survivorship options. Typical Survivorship options include a 50% and 100% option. There may also be an option for a custom option where you request data for a specific percentage survivorship option like 75% or 25%.

So what are the implications for these different options?

Single Life Annuity

This will provide you with the highest monthly benefit amount for the rest of your life. Typically, unless there is some kind of unique provision in the plan, when you die the income stream stops. So, if you live a long time, great, you chose wisely. If you die a year after retirement, you chose poorly because in theory the pension fund "owes" your family payments until you would have reached average life expectancy; but you died early and thus the income stops. Obviously we don't know for sure how long you will live after you retire so often when the Single Life Annuity is chosen, the retiree is either:

1) Single with nobody to protect financially in the event of their early death in retirement.
2) Wealthy enough that even if they died early in retirement their surviving spouse wouldn't have to worry about money. They are assuming that they will live to an advanced age.
3) Implementing a Pension Maximization Strategy. We will discuss this later.

Survivorship Options

Married couples generally lean toward choosing a survivorship option of some kind.

You will take a lower monthly payment in exchange for a continuation of payments to your survivor (spouse usually) in the event that you die first. The higher the survivorship percentage you choose, the lower your monthly payment becomes. For example, if you choose the 100% survivor option, when you die your survivor will get 100% of what you were getting for the rest of their life. They get the same paycheck you were getting.

If you pick the 50% option, your survivor will get 50% or half of what your paycheck was every month until they die. Obviously, it would stand to reason that if you request a 100% option over a 50% option, that your pension payment would be reduced to a greater degree to offset the liability of the pension fund being on the hook to pay out 100% to your survivor instead of just 50%, got it?

So, why does the pension fund care what the age and gender of your survivor is? They plug this information into a mortality table to figure out the probability of having to pay survivor benefits and for how long. This will affect how much your pension payment is reduced to provide survivor benefits to your spouse.

For example, if you are a woman teacher and your husband (survivor) is 10 years older than you, your monthly pension benefit probably won't be significantly affected if you choose a survivorship option. Why? Chances are he is going to die before you. He is 10 years older and men tend to die earlier than women, so he has two strikes against him. (www.scientificamerican.com)

Now let's switch up the roles. Let's say you are a male teacher and your wife (survivor) is 10 years younger than you. Now we have issues. You will notice that your pension benefit will likely be greatly reduced to provide survivorship benefits to your wife because she will probably outlive you considerably. Single men are hot commodities in the old folks home, right?

Most people will feel the need to provide for their spouse in the event that they die first. Usually this leads to strong consideration of choosing a survivorship option. However, the decision is not always that simple. Let's say you pick a survivorship option to protect your spouse. Because you are picking this option, your monthly pension check is now $500 less than if you were to pick the Single Life option. What happens if your spouse dies first? Oops, never thought of that. Well, in most cases your choice was irrevocable and you cannot change it. So now you are out $500 per month for the rest of your life and your survivor is dead. That benefit is now worthless. Enter the Pension Maximization Strategy.

Pension Maximization Strategy

Very simply, what you do is choose the Single Life Option and buy life insurance to protect your spouse financially. You pay the premiums for this insurance with the difference between what you would receive under the Single Life option, and what you would have received if a Survivorship Option had been chosen. Usually, you would want permanent insurance so it doesn't lapse, but in some cases we combine a permanent policy with a term policy. This provides a larger pool of death benefit money in the early retirement years so that if you die early your spouse has a larger pool of money to draw from. Later on in retirement, the term will expire, leaving just the permanent policy. The thought process is that your spouse would be reaching advanced age at that point and would need fewer assets to support them until their eventual death. You would typically name your spouse as the primary beneficiary and the children as contingent beneficiaries on the policies. Ok, so now we know in basic terms how to structure a pension maximization plan. It is important to note that this strategy is contingent upon being able to find sufficient life insurance coverage at a premium level that is covered by the extra monthly income from the single life option. Now let's go over why this can be so attractive.

There are four basic scenarios that can happen to a married couple regarding death in retirement:

1) You can die first, die early, and your spouse lives on for decades.
2) You can die together (car accident, etc.)
3) You can die first but at an advanced age; in this case your spouse would be shortly behind you (unless your spouse is much younger, in which case, good for you!)
4) Your spouse can die first.

In the first scenario, you die first and early, and your spouse lives a long time afterward. If you pick a survivorship option from the pension this could be a good choice because your spouse would receive survivorship benefits for many years. However, you don't know when you are going to die, and who is going to die first.

In the second scenario you both die together. In the event that you picked a survivorship option, the income stops because you are both dead. If you would have done a pension maximization strategy, your children, other family members, or charity would be named as contingent beneficiaries on the life insurance so they would get the proceeds. If your circumstances allow for this, it can be a much better outcome than picking a survivorship option.

In scenario three, you die first but at an advanced age. Ok, if you would have picked a survivorship option, yes, your spouse would get benefits. But only for a year or so until they ultimately die too, at which point the income would end. The kids, family members, or charity get nothing. To add insult to injury, most likely the pension plan will not have a cost of living adjustment, so that one or two years' worth of survivorship payments have been eroded by inflation for thirty years or so, and are worth a fraction of what they originally were.

If you chose a pension maximization strategy, you would have many more options available. You could have removed your spouse as primary beneficiary when you started reaching advanced age and simply named the children to create an inheritance or legacy. You could have gifted them the policy, or you could have simply surrendered it for the cash value and used the money while you were still alive. Lots of options.

In the last scenario, your spouse pre-deceases you. This is where the real beauty of the strategy comes into play. If you chose a survivorship option, you would have locked into a lower pension payment for the rest of your life and your spouse/survivor is now dead. Tough luck.

If you would have done a pension maximization strategy you would now have lots of options. First, you can stop paying the premiums on your life insurance and surrender the policies to get any cash value. You can think of this as a partial refund of the premiums you paid. So now you are receiving the full Single Life annuity payment from your pension and it is now unencumbered by any life insurance premiums. Another choice would be to keep the insurance and make the kids your primary beneficiaries therefore ensuring a legacy to them. You could also choose to reduce the amount of insurance that you have thereby reducing or possibly eliminating your premium payments and still leaving a smaller inheritance to the kids. By the way, since life insurance proceeds are generally income tax free, it is a great vehicle to transfer wealth to the next generation.

In most scenarios it is to your advantage to use a pension maximization strategy. The only scenario that can give it a run for its money is if you die first and die early, and your survivor lives a very long time. In this case picking a survivorship option would have turned out to be a good choice.

Some of you may have figured this out already, but it is very important so I am making it clear here. A lot of teachers happen to marry other teachers. If you AND your spouse have pensions, a pension maximization strategy should be seriously considered. You see, there is a 100% chance that either you or your spouse will pre-decease the other if you do not die together. Think about that for a second. So if either of you or both of you pick survivorship options, at least one of you, if not both of you, is guaranteed to pick the wrong option.

I have never had a client say that they didn't like the idea of pension maximization. The problem is that most people have never heard of this and do not understand it. Now you do. Some challenges that arise from this strategy come from medical underwriting for the life insurance. A lot of people try to implement this strategy in the year before retirement. At that age, they're likely to have medical conditions that can make obtaining a good health rating difficult or impossible. One way to pre-plan for this type of strategy is to get term insurance with a convertibility feature earlier in life while you are still in great health. A convertibility feature allows you to convert some or all of your term insurance to permanent coverage without any medical underwriting. So if you originally received a preferred health rating on your term insurance when you were 40, you could convert it at age 60 to permanent coverage with a preferred rating regardless of how poor your current condition may be. By getting a term policy earlier, you are ensuring your insurability for later.

It is critical to work with someone who knows what they are doing here to make sure you acquire quality insurance that will do what you want it to do. You will also need guidance when choosing the right amount of insurance and in deciding if you should combine term and permanent coverage in your plan or simply use permanent insurance. A pension maximization strategy is a powerful tool that can help to increase your income in retirement if your spouse predeceases you, or to help pass wealth to the next generation.

Retirement Plans: 403(b), 457(b), 401(k), 401(a), IRA's, Roth IRA's, Annuities

As you transition into retirement you probably have a collection of different retirement accounts that you have accumulated over the years. Your spouse might have a collection as well. These different accounts may be 403(b), 457(b), 401(k), 401(a), IRA's, Roth IRA's, Cash Balance Plans, and annuities of varying flavors. So what the heck do we do with this mess? I mean, c'mon! The mail that you get from all these investment companies is stacked up six-inches on your kitchen counter.

Typically, in retirement there is a desire to simplify life and consolidate these accounts as much as possible. Many pre-tax accounts can be rolled over or transferred into one another. This would be 403(b), 401(k), Cash Balance plans, 401(a), and Traditional pretax IRA's. While it may seem tempting to just combine EVERYTHING, you should use care when consolidating all of your accounts together. Some may have unique benefits or provisions that you would be giving up like higher guaranteed interest rates, or guaranteed withdraw benefits if you close the account. Also, some may levy surrender charges or penalties if you liquidate them before a certain period of time.

Some accounts have unique IRS withdraw provisions. For example, you can access money from a 403(b) or 401(k) without incurring the IRS's 10% early withdraw penalty at age 55 or older and severed from service from your employer, while you generally cannot access money out of an IRA until age 59.5 without making use of a strategy called a 72(t) distribution which locks you into making withdraws for the later of five years or until you reach 59.5. This is usually not ideal, particularly if you just need cash for a one-time event and do not need to consistently draw income. 72(t) distribution planning can be very sophisticated and is beyond the scope of this book. Let's just say that if you retire at 57 years old and want to take a bit of money out of a retirement plan for a trip or vacation, it would be much more in your best interest to take it out of a 403(b) than an IRA because you could access it without penalty (www.irs.gov). The age 55 and severed from service provision applies to 403(b) and 401(k) accounts, but not IRAs.

Also, if you remember from the beginning of the book (I don't blame you if you don't) 457(b)'s simply have a severance from service provision to access the money without IRS penalty. There is no age provision (www.irs.gov). So as you can see, it is extremely important to work with a knowledgeable advisor to make sure that you aren't giving up something beneficial just to consolidate accounts. That being said, to the extent that it makes sense, consolidating as much as possible will simplify your life in the future as far as getting fewer account statements, having a better handle on where your money is and how the total overall portfolio is invested, and may make things a bit easier when you have to start taking money out of your accounts at age 70.5 for your required minimum distributions (RMD). More on RMD's in a bit.

So if you retire before age 59.5 it could very well be in your best interest to keep some of your money in a 403(b) or 457(b) plan so you have money to access before age 59.5 when your IRA balances will become available to you free of any IRS early withdraw penalties. A word to the wise; even if you don't think you will need to touch those accounts before age 59.5 you never know what life will throw your way. It is always better to have access and not use the funds, than not to have penalty free access and need to use the funds.

So, if we have some funds ear-marked for possible early access in 403(b) or 457(b) plans then we can consider consolidating the rest into an IRA. If you are already 59.5 or older, there is no benefit of a 403(b), 401(k), or 457(b) from a perspective of withdraw accessibility so it is six in one hand, a half dozen in the other whether you have your money in a 403(b) or IRA.

While we are talking about consolidation of accounts, I thought I would bring up a question that I am frequently asked. "Can I roll-over my spouse's IRA, 401(k), etc. into MY IRA, 403(b), etc.?" Nope. Retirement accounts are individual and cannot be commingled among spouses. Actually, IRA stands for Individual Retirement Account.

We discussed the tax treatment of all of these accounts in the first part of the book, but to quickly recap: all pre-tax plans such as 403(b), 401(k), IRA and 457(b) grow tax deferred and taxes are ultimately owed when you take money out of the accounts. So now you pay the piper. If you are not currently taking distributions from these plans in order to avoid the taxes, the government will require you to take distributions from your account by April 1 of the year after the year in which you turn 70.5. Why? They want their tax money. One quick caveat to mention: if you are still working at 70.5 or older you do not have to take RMD's from your employer sponsored plan. You will have to take them from your IRA's though. So as a possible planning point, you could rollover or transfer your IRA balances into your 403(b) and put off RMD's until you stop working entirely and get a couple more years of tax deferred accumulation. When you do start taking money out of your pre-tax accounts, the distributions will be taxable just like earned income or salary.

You can generally take distributions however you choose from these accounts. Some people choose to have a certain dollar amount sent to them automatically each month directly into their bank account, some choose to take withdraws as they need the money on a less structured basis, some do a combination of the two.

While I am not saying this will describe you, what I see a lot of with retired teachers is that their pension income and Social Security is high enough in the early years of retirement that there is no need to set up automatic monthly drafts from their investment accounts. They tend to take bits and pieces here and there for unexpected expenses, holidays, vacations, etc. When they get a little further along in retirement and inflation has eroded the purchasing power of their pensions, they start to set up automatic monthly drafts from their investments. Obviously, once they hit 70.5 we have to start taking income.

Roth Accounts

Roth accounts whether 401(k), 403(b) or IRA will accumulate tax free and with certain qualifications met, will ultimately be distributed tax free. These accounts should generally be liquidated last due to their powerful tax free structure and also because there are no Required Minimum Distribution mandates with these accounts.

Taxable Accounts (stocks, bonds, mutual funds, ETF's, etc.)

As we covered earlier in the book, liquidating these investments may subject you to capital gains or dividend tax, ordinary income tax, or both. Usually, in retirement these accounts should be liquidated first, before pre-tax accounts and Roth accounts, due to their lack of tax deferred or tax free growth.

Real Estate (rental, investment, downsizing of house for equity, reverse mortgage)

You may also generate income from real estate during retirement. Maybe you invested in a rental or vacation property while you were working and it is now generating positive cash flow each month. Maybe you invested in real estate and decide to sell it in retirement. Many people will decide to downsize their house in retirement for ease of maintenance and lower overhead costs. In so doing you might realize a bit of profit that can generate some income for you in retirement. Finally, some may choose to look into a reverse mortgage. I am not going to get into the details here, but as an overview this is a way for certain people to stay in your house and get equity out of it while you are still alive. If this strategy is of interest to you, please contact a qualified professional to assess your individual situation.

Part-Time work/Second Career

Many people will decide to work part-time in retirement. If you are thinking of retiring in your late 50s or early-to-mid 60s, you will find that you are still very young and have a need to do something on a regular basis. You might miss the social interaction, or feel a need to belong and contribute to something. Maybe you just always wanted to work on your hobby but it was never possible when you were raising a family.

Part-time work in retirement is great because it solves all of those issues. It can keep you mentally sharp, physically active and socially involved. It also generates a paycheck. This can allow you to splurge on some purchases you may otherwise not have bought. It could also help you delay Social Security, therefore bringing you a larger Social Security payment every month. Many people will consider it and are very happy when they do decide to work part time.

Chapter 8 Points to Remember

- Many people will benefit from waiting until full retirement age to collect Social Security due to the larger monthly benefit and the COLA attached.
- Pensions will provide a large portion of the monthly income for many of the teachers who are reading this book.
- If you need to financially protect a spouse, consider a pension maximization strategy.
- 403(b), 401(k) and 457(b) plans provide for penalty free withdraws earlier than IRA's. If you are considering retirement before 59.5, you may want to consider leaving funds in these accounts.
- You must make Required Minimum Distributions from IRA's and other pre-tax retirement plans by April 1 of the year after the year in which you reach age 70.5.
- Generally speaking, when you start to take withdraws in retirement you should liquidate your taxable accounts first, then pre-tax accounts, and lastly your Roth accounts.
- Part time work can be very rewarding from financial, mental, physical, and social aspects.

CHAPTER 9

Planning for Sustainable Income Streams in Retirement

There has been a lot of discussion particularly among the baby boomer generation about distribution planning in retirement. Actually, the biggest concern for most baby boomers is that they are deathly afraid that they will run out of money in retirement. I cannot stress enough that this is a very serious topic and you should get help from a competent advisor. Major expenses like healthcare costs and long-term care issues can easily throw a plan off track if they have not been addressed and planned for.

What I will do is give you an overview of how to plan for these income streams so you can be better educated when you are working with your advisor. As I mentioned earlier it is critically important to get a good idea of what your monthly expenses are and if any expenses are expected to increase or decrease materially in the future.

Next we can add up all the fixed income sources in the household like pensions and Social Security. We need to calculate what the after tax income will be from these sources and compare that to what our monthly recurring expenses are. If we have an excess of income over expenses, we are in good shape. If we have an excess of expenses over income, we have some work to do.

What I prefer to do is plan for guaranteed income sources to cover the monthly recurring expenses. This is a strategy called "flooring." We are making an income floor to ensure that all the fixed and/or regular and recurring expenses can be paid each month. If there is an income shortfall, sometimes we will use some of our investments and savings to buy an annuity. This annuity will provide the guaranteed income to bridge the gap. In the strictest sense, an annuity is a promise from an insurance company to make a series of payments to you for the rest of your life or a certain number of years in exchange for a sum of money. As I mentioned in the first part of this book there are many annuities these days, all with different benefits, cost structures, guarantees, and bells and whistles. It's important to remember that all guarantees in an annuity are backed by the claims-paying ability of the issuing company, so it is important to work with a reputable, highly rated company and a trustworthy, knowledgeable advisor.

Another strategy is to take withdraws from the investment portfolio using a sustainable withdraw rate. A lot of research has gone into figuring out what this withdraw rate is. I am not going to bore you with the research, but a widely suggested withdraw rate is roughly 4% of the portfolio in the beginning year (www.schwab.com). Some experts say that you can take out more and some say that you should take out less, but 4% can be a good starting place. You can adjust it up for inflation every following year. Many believe this strategy can help ensure that you will not run out of money before you die. Being a bit more cautious than some, I also recommend that if the market is having a particularly bad year that you reduce the withdraw amount a little bit in that year.

I should say that if you are significantly younger than normal retirement age, you should consider taking a lesser than 4% initial withdraw and if you are much older than normal retirement age, you very well might be able to get away with a higher withdraw rate because your remaining life expectancy is shorter.

While taking all of that into consideration, let's just use the 4% to give you an idea of how much you can withdraw safely from your accounts. For those of you who are jumping ahead, yeah, it's not a lot of money. If you have $1,000,000, congratulations! You did a great job saving over your lifetime. However, you are not yet Jed Clampett from the "Beverly Hillbillies". A $1,000,000 account will generate about $40,000 per year, or $3,333 monthly BEFORE TAXES. Figure somewhere around $2,600 monthly after the tax man has his share. Remember, you will be able to give yourself a cost of living adjustment raise on this number each year, but it is still a much smaller annual income than most people initially expect.

The reason I detail this is because a lot of people think that they can safely take out a much higher percentage of their money each year in retirement. You might even be thinking "Wait, if my investments return about 10% annually, can't I take out $100,000 from my $1,000,000 every year and never touch my principal?" No, you can't. Here's why.

Sequence of Returns.

Due to stock market volatility the actual rates of return or interest rates can be vastly different in each year. This volatility greatly impacts the amount we can safely take out. If you have a series of years early in retirement when the market does well, then you will likely be in good shape throughout retirement and probably have money left over when you die. However, if the opposite happens, you could run out of money very early and have to go back to work or make significant changes to your income plan.

Here is a quick example. Let's use that $1,000,000 account for simplicity. We are going to assume a 10% withdraw rate based on historic market yields. It seems logical, right?

Year 1: $1,000,000- $100,000= $900,000 assume that the market is flat—basically a zero percent rate of return.

Year 2: $900,000-$100,000 and the market is down around 10%= $720,000

Year 3: $720,000-$100,000 and the market is down around 5%= $589,000

Year 4: $589,000-$100,000 and the market is flat again= $489,000

Ok, so looking at that example, I certainly did not paint a doomsday scenario, right? One year of flat returns, one year of 10% loss, one year of 5% loss, and then another flat year. But look at the account value after the 4th year. $489,000. Oops, guess who is going back to work? You would need over a 100% rate of return to bring you back up to $1,000,000! To add insult to injury, you still have income needs from your money. This is nearly impossible to recover from. Stick with around 4% for the withdraw rate and most importantly, work with an advisor to structure your income streams so that they are sustainable over your and your spouse's retirement.

I think it is very important to consider staying invested in the stock market throughout your retirement. The amount of cash flow that you have coming in from fixed income sources such as pensions, Social Security, and annuities will to some degree influence how much of your portfolio you can allocate to stocks. Everybody's personal situation is different, and everybody's risk tolerance is different, so work with a good advisor to decide what may be appropriate for you.

Remember, over long periods of time stocks tend to outperform bonds and cash. However, stocks also tend to have added volatility. Because of this you don't want to have all of your savings in stocks. If the market does undergo a large correction and you need money you may be forced to sell some of your investments at a loss. Also remember that being well diversified helps to smooth out the ups and downs of the markets. You should still have exposure to a diverse range of investments such as large-, mid-, and small-size US funds, and Developed and Emerging Markets International funds.

To look at it another way, it's not a bad idea to have about a year or two's worth of cash needs in fixed income investments (cash and various bonds) just to help ride out the fluctuations in the stock market. If you have much more than that in fixed income; I think you may be missing out on some opportunities while you are in retirement. I think that too many people see retirement as the end of the game, while I like to look at it more like half-time. Most people will spend a long time in retirement and will have a need to continue accumulating their assets throughout.

So to recap, I usually will recommend the use of an annuity or annuities to plan for enough guaranteed income in retirement in connection with Social Security and pension income. This creates confidence knowing that we have planned to not run out of income for the rest of our lives even if the worst case scenario happens and we run out of money in our investment accounts. Once we have the income streams from annuities properly structured, we can take withdraws from our investment accounts in a sustainable manner so that we have a high probability of not running out of money before death.

Peace of mind and confidence in retirement can and should be increased by addressing the big issues like healthcare and long-term care with insurance. A serious medical issue can have a devastating effect on assets and income streams in retirement. Also, taking measures to reduce debt, thereby decreasing monthly expenses, helps tremendously so that we do not need as many assets to generate higher income streams.

Chapter 9 Points to Remember

- Consider annuities to plan for guaranteed income streams in retirement.
- Studies indicate that a sustainable withdraw rate in most portfolios is somewhere around 4% annually with an inflation adjustment each year.
- Sequence of returns is why the safe withdraw rate is so low. If you have a couple bad years in the market early in retirement and you are withdrawing a high rate you can deplete a portfolio quickly.
- Retirement is not the end of the game; it is more like half time. There is still a need for accumulation in your portfolio.

CHAPTER 10

LEGACY PLANNING AND ESTATE PLANNING

At some point, everybody has to plan for their own death. Nobody has been able to escape it yet. While we talked quite a bit about insurance planning and estate planning in the earlier chapters, we focused primarily on dying before you are "supposed" to die. Now I'd like to focus on estate planning and transfer of wealth if you die when you are supposed to die in your 80s or 90s.

First, I will mention that if you die first and are survived by your spouse, unless you specifically indicate in your will and beneficiary designations, your property is not assured to transfer to your spouse. Many assume that their spouse will automatically get everything: this is not true. Also, if you have children from another marriage or otherwise want to provide for parties other than your current spouse, I would strongly recommend that you meet with a qualified estate planning attorney to make sure that your legal documents are structured so that what you want to happen actually happens.

What I want to focus on in this section is transferring wealth to the next generation and/or charities.

Some of us may pass without many assets. In this case, there is not much of a need for sophisticated estate planning strategies. Frankly, we won't be getting into these strategies anyway because it is beyond the scope of this book. Some of us, however, may pass with significant assets. These assets can be in the form of retirement plans, real estate, savings, and brokerage account balances. Of course there can also be life insurance death benefits.

Your estate is all of your property that you own or control during your lifetime and at the time of your death. There are two types of property; real and personal. Personal property can either be tangible or intangible. Real Property is land and anything that is attached to the land. Personal Property is anything that is not real property—cars, boats, and diamonds being of the tangible (touchable, movable) type, and trade secrets, copyrights, bonds, stocks, etc., being intangible (unable to move or touch).

It is said that there are three groups that can receive your estate after you die. Your family, charity, or the government. The planning that you do will largely determine to what degree these different parties receive your estate.

As was previously mentioned, it is imperative that you have a will and that it is up to date. This is to help ensure that your wishes are followed as to whom gets your property. It is also very important throughout your life to make sure that your beneficiary designations on retirement plans and life insurance contracts are up to date and accurate. Accounts with a named beneficiary will override what your will states so be aware of this. It is not enough to change your will if you have a life change or simply change your mind about the disposition of your assets. You must make sure that all of your named beneficiaries have been updated as well.

Some of you may be best served to speak with an estate planning attorney about setting up a living trust. These can be both revocable and irrevocable. In most basic terms, there is a grantor, a trustee, and beneficiaries of the trust. The grantor is the person who transfers the property into the trust. In this case we'll say the grantor is you. You take your property and re-title it in the name of the trust. There is also the trustee of the trust. Typically, this would also be you during your lifetime if using a revocable trust, and perhaps your spouse or a child would be set up as successor trustee in the event you become incapacitated or die. The trustee simply administers the trust according to the trust terms. Think of this kind of like an executor of an estate. Lastly, there is the beneficiary or beneficiaries of the trust. They are the parties who receive the property at death. This will typically be the children, grandchildren, and possibly charities if so inclined.

Arguably, the main benefit of a revocable living trust is to pass property to heirs bypassing probate. Probate is the process of filing your will (typically in the county of your residence). This procedure notifies creditors of your estate and appoints the executor. It is done through a state probate court and is basically the process of paying off any outstanding debts and then transferring the rest of the assets to heirs. Probate can be a long and potentially costly process. Titling assets in a living trust can help to avoid the probate process. For those with property in different states, this can be very helpful because your estate property would be subject to probate in multiple states. Not fun!

Other benefits of revocable living trusts include:

1) Speeding up the process of transferring property.
2) Reducing the cost of administration.
3) Adding a level of privacy to the process. Once your will is in probate it is public information.
4) Helping with issues of diminished capacity. You can name a successor trustee and include provisions for when a successor trustee will take over.

Did you notice that I didn't include a fifth benefit claiming "they reduce taxes"? There is a huge misconception among a lot of people that revocable living trusts reduce taxes. They don't. Titling your assets in a revocable living trust does not remove the assets from your estate. Please do not make this mistake.

Most living trusts for this audience would be set up as revocable living trusts. As such you still have control over the assets in the trust and can make changes when and how you see fit. The downside would be that the assets are still part of your estate and may be subject to federal estate tax. However, for 2015 the Federal Estate tax exemption is over $5.43 million per spouse so you would need to have an estate worth around $11,000,000 or more, if married, to have a Federal Estate Tax problem. Be aware that the estate tax exclusion has been lower in the past, and can change at any time in the future so just because you don't have a Federal Estate Tax problem now doesn't mean that you won't in the future.

Irrevocable living trusts transfer the assets out of the estate so they are not subject to federal and state death taxes. However, you give away all control of the assets by doing so. Typically, these trusts are used by the ultra-high net worth, and I am really only mentioning them here for completeness. Revocable living trusts will represent almost all of the living trusts used by retired teachers, even the affluent and higher net worth teachers and their families.

Pre-Tax Retirement Accounts

Pre-tax retirement accounts like IRAs, 403(b)'s, 401(k)'s, and the like will pass onto the named beneficiaries and therefore aren't part of the probate process. (I mentioned earlier in the book, but it is worth saying again; please make sure that you update your beneficiary designations and that they coordinate with your will. Remember, a named beneficiary will override what you indicate in your will. If you want to make sure that your ex-husband (or whomever) from 20 years ago doesn't get your retirement account or life insurance upon your death, please make sure you don't still have him listed as a beneficiary on your accounts.) The beneficiaries of these accounts, typically children, will have the option to take the funds and pay income tax, or to "stretch" the required minimum distributions (RMD) over THEIR lifetimes in "inherited" accounts. This can be a tremendous wealth extender particularly if there are large balances in the plans. In my experience, most people who inherit small IRAs, say up to $50,000ish, simply take the money from the account, pay the taxes and move on. It's less to deal with than taking RMD's for a small account like that. However, for those who inherit say $250,000 in an IRA, it could very well be in their best interest to "stretch" out the RMD's for as long as they can and let the account continue to grow tax deferred. The additional concern if they were to take all $250,000 at once would be that it would spike their income for that year and potentially push them into a higher tax bracket.

Roth IRA's

Roth IRA's can either be distributed by December 31 of the fifth year following the year of the owner's death (5-year rule); or distributed over the remaining life of the beneficiary by taking RMD's (www.irs. gov).

Taxable Accounts

Investments held in taxable accounts receive a step up in cost basis for those who inherit the assets so there will be no capital gains tax. For a very basic example, let's say you bought XYZ mutual fund for $20 per share back when you were 30 years old and you are now in your 80s. $20 is your cost basis (how much you originally bought it for). When you die, say in your mid-80s, it is worth $2000 (remember compound interest? Isn't that crazy?!)

If you would have sold that mutual fund during your lifetime you would have realized a capital gain of $1980 and had to pay capital gains tax on that amount. However, you died holding the fund; now it's a different situation. Your estate will receive a step up in cost basis to the value on the date of death, $2,000. So at that point there is no capital gains tax owed, and your heirs will inherit that mutual fund with a cost basis of $2,000 (www.investopedia.com). Cool, huh? As an important note, if you gift away the assets during your lifetime, the recipient of the gift will maintain the original cost basis.

Life Insurance

Life insurance death benefit proceeds are the Granddaddy of them all. These are generally received 100% income tax free by the beneficiary. Because there is a named beneficiary they also bypass probate too, remember? As a matter of fact, life insurance is probably the most popular and efficient way to create a legacy or to transfer wealth due to its tax free payout.

Some people may consider buying a permanent life insurance policy naming the children, grandchildren, or trust as beneficiary just to guarantee that they leave an inheritance for the next generation. Some people will find themselves in a situation in retirement where they have more money than they will reasonably be able to spend. They may consider utilizing some of their assets to pay the premiums on a life insurance policy to more efficiently transfer wealth. If someone does not need the income from their required minimum distributions from retirement plans, they may decide to use the RMD's to pay premiums on a life insurance policy and leverage that wealth.

It is very important to make a key differentiation here. The life insurance is not at all being used for financial protection. In this situation, the people already have more money than they need and the "kids" are likely in their 50s and 60s. The life insurance plays another role entirely; it is simply being used to efficiently transfer wealth, income tax free, outside of probate. It is worth noting that more and more people are starting to view life insurance as a different asset class in their portfolio, just like stocks and bonds.

Unfortunately, all too often people procrastinate their estate planning. You've worked hard for a long time to build what you have. Please take the relatively short amount of time to meet with an estate planning attorney, elder law attorney, and qualified financial planner to make sure that everything is set up properly and in the most tax efficient way possible. Remember, there are three parties that can inherit your estate after you die; your family, charity, or the government. I'm willing to bet I know which one you least prefer.

Chapter 10 Points to Remember

- Everybody eventually dies. You will not be first one to escape it. Make sure you do not procrastinate your estate planning.
- If you are the first spouse to die, provided you took the necessary steps to affect this, your spouse can take over as owner of all of your property.
- After the second spouse dies, it is largely up to the planning that you did to determine whether your family, charity, or the government gets your assets.
- Make sure that you have a will and that it is up to date and accurate.
- Accounts with a named beneficiary such as retirement accounts and life insurance pass directly to the beneficiary outside of probate. Make sure your beneficiary designations are correct.
- You may want to discuss with an estate planning attorney whether a living trust would be appropriate.
- Retirement plans like 403(b), 401(k), and IRA can be stretched over the lifetime of the beneficiary. This can be a great wealth builder.
- Investments in taxable accounts receive a step up in cost basis at death.
- Life insurance proceeds are generally income tax free and can be a great way to leverage and transfer wealth to the next generation or charity.

AFTERWORD

Well, I think that's about it. I really hope that you learned a lot and enjoyed reading my book. I've spent my whole career working with teachers and their families helping to explain these concepts in terms that they can easily understand. While there are some differences between the different state pension plans and differences between public schools and private schools and higher education, the information that I give in this book is applicable to everybody.

What I have learned throughout my career having thousands of meetings with teachers is that teachers are overwhelmingly warm, caring people. They are highly intelligent, but also terribly overworked. They want to understand this stuff, but they just don't have the time. They need somebody to explain it to them so they can feel confident starting to work with an advisor to create a plan.

Does this book include everything about everything? No way. It was never meant to. That book would be 1000 pages long and nobody would even start to read it. The mission of this book was to give you 90% of what you need to know, and I feel that it does just that. If you got value out of this book, please encourage your colleagues and your friends to get a copy- spread the word. I feel that it's important for every teacher in the country to possess this basic knowledge. Pay it forward and get a copy for the new teacher down the hall or your friends in your building. It can make an inexpensive holiday present for the teachers in your life.

Throughout the book I have indicated the need to work with a competent advisor. If you currently have one, great! I hope this book will help you communicate and collaborate easier with your advisor.

If you would like to inquire about working with me and my firm Educated Wealth Strategies, please visit WWW. EDUCATEDWEALTHSTRATEGIES.COM for more information on our services. We have the ability to work with clients all over the country and have advisors who can work with teachers at all stages of the planning process whether you are in your first year or your last. We also have a ton of free additional resources on our site like newsletters, articles, and calculators, so check it out.

ABOUT THE AUTHOR

Eric Nichols started his career in financial services in 2003 after being recruited by AXA Advisors from Villanova University. His financial planning practice has always been focused on the needs of educators and their families. Today Eric works primarily with educators nearing retirement and High Net Worth and affluent educators and their families. Many of his clients include multiple generations of family members. Because many of the spouses of his teacher clients are business owners, physicians, attorneys and corporate executives he is very well versed in the planning needs of these professionals as well. He serves as the President of Educated Wealth Strategies; a comprehensive wealth management firm focused on the needs of teachers and their families. Eric is recognized as one of the most successful advisors in the country.

Eric's professional education and knowledge is extensive. In addition to his finance degree from Villanova University he is a CERTIFIED FINANCIAL PLANNER™ professional (CFP®), Chartered Life Underwriter (CLU®), Retirement Income Certified Professional (RICP®), and a Chartered Retirement Planning Counselor (CRPC®).

Eric lives in the greater Philadelphia area with his wife and two sons. In his free time, he enjoys spending time with his family, playing golf (poorly), outdoor sports, and he is an avid CrossFitter.

33321109R00082

Made in the USA
Middletown, DE
08 July 2016